T0149354

Nothing
is
Forever

A Memoir Collection of Short Stories

iUniverse, Inc.
Bloomington

NOTHING IS FOREVER
A Memoir Collection of Short Stories

iUniverse books may be ordered through booksellers or by contacting:

iUniverse
1663 Liberty Drive
Bloomington, IN 47403
www.iuniverse.com
1-800-Authors (1-800-288-4677)

ISBN: 978-1-4759-2731-3 (sc)
ISBN: 978-1-4759-2732-0 (ebk)

Printed in the United States of America

iUniverse rev. date: 06/20/2012

TABLE OF CONTENTS

THE EARLY YEARS

SUSIE AND JEFFREY

BITS AND PIECES

Jeffrey
Thank you for your love and constant support
I will always love you

Ali
The love of my life

Susie
No day goes by without my thinking of you
I will love you forever

Acknowledgments

Madonna Dries Christensen entered my life from out of the blue. I advise my students to not use trite statements . . . however; this one is true. She's an angel, something else I don't believe in . . . but she is, for me. Her help in editing and guiding me throughout this process has been enormous.

Bill Andrews and I met over a decade ago in a Writing Workshop at Lifelong Learning Academy (LLA). He is my friend and editor. Bill knows where I should put the period and eliminate the comma. Then, patiently he asks, "Helga, do you need that sentence?"

Jeffrey Harris and **Alan Kranich,** my computer gurus, who are always available to me . . . day and night. They are angels, too.

Barbara Lupoff, my "in-house" librarian . . . she's better than spell-check. My calls are welcome at any time.

Special thanks to my colleagues in the **Writing Workshop of LLA.** They have encouraged me to read bits and pieces of this collection. Their input has been invaluable.

THE
EARLY
YEARS

They Called Us Little Jewish Bitches

It was Berlin, April 1938; Hitler's Germany.

Ruth and I were ten years old.

The day before we left Berlin forever, my parents finally permitted me to tell Ruth and her family about our departure. *Forever? FOREVER!*

I see her still at the train station. She had a sweet, round face with rosy cheeks and blond curls escaping out of her wool hat. Ruth was short and chubby . . . like a dumpling. On that day the weather was unusually clear and cool. She wore a pleated skirt, white blouse and a hand knitted sweater. Like typical Jewish girls in Berlin, her hair was short. Aryan girls wore their hair in two long braids, a single plait, or twisted on top of their heads like crowns. Most German girls were blond and blue-eyed, but that was also true of a great number of Jewish girls. We could have "passed." To this day I wonder, *why didn't we wear our hair long . . . to assimilate in order not to be such easy targets?*

Ruth was my very best friend. We had been inseparable since we were five years old . . . almost a lifetime. We

1

met in Kindergarten. Coincidentally, we both had brothers five years our senior, and longed for a sister . . . having none . . . we adopted each other.

From the first day we attended school we sat next to each other. Through our friendship our mothers became friends. They were very formal, addressing each other by their surnames, even after many years. On weekends and holidays they frequently took us ice-skating, to puppet shows, the zoo, children's theater and other entertainment appropriate for our age. Ruth and I, of course, enjoyed Shirley Temple movies.

What I loved best were the Sundays when our mothers took us to the afternoon café at *KaDeWe*, the largest, most elegant department store in Berlin. Ruth and I dressed in our finest for these occasions. I felt special and grown up. Usually we had hot chocolate with mountains of *Schlagsahne,* (whipped cream) fruit tarts or ice cream. We were not permitted ice cream in the winter . . . it was believed to cause colds when consumed out of season.

When our mothers met for a *Kaffe Klatsch* with their own friends, Ruth and I usually had our own table nearby. We were able to chat and dream about wearing shoes with little high heels and dance dresses when we got a bit older. Quietly we giggled, and when we got bored we went into the ladies' room. There were always several attendants who kept themselves busy folding cloth napkins like origami. Ruth and I were fascinated. The women were amused by our enthusiasm, and taught us their craft.

Our families didn't live on the same street, but it was only a ten-minute walk between our homes. For years our maids met at a designated corner and walked us to school.

Ella had been our sleep-in-maid since I was three years old. Everyone in my family loved her. My mother's relationship with Ella was close. She treated her like a relative and helped her accumulate a trousseau, and promised to pay for her wedding in the future.

I remember her proudly taking me into her room to show me the marvelous linens she was saving in the handcrafted wooden hope chest at the foot of her bed.

We were devastated when Hitler ruled that Aryan females under the age of thirty-five were no longer permitted to work as sleep-in-maids for Jewish families. The goodbyes to our loyal and loving Ella were heart breaking. Frau Sasse, an older woman, was hired as a day worker to replace her. She was pleasant but no comparison to our Ella. Frau Sasse obviously trusted my parents since she confided in them about her unhappiness with Hitler. Her teenage grandson was forced to join the Nazi Youth Party. If he had not "volunteered," he would not have been able to find employment in the future, and his family would have been in jeopardy.

Our walks to school were happy times. The maids gossiped behind us, and Ruth and I giggled, as little girls did, but not too loudly. We indulged in the typical girl talk of ten-year-olds, but were always aware of possibly being watched by Nazis . . . wearing swastika armbands on their immaculate uniforms. They made lots of noise stomping their high leather boots when marching on the cobblestone streets. Hearing their thunderous steps approaching was frightening. A normal carefree childhood did not exist for us because of Hitler. We were always on alert when outside the safety of our home. School was serious with strict rules and regulations. Since Jewish children were no longer permitted to attend the German public schools, we went to a private institution sponsored by a Jewish organization.

Ruth's sparkling blue eyes always brightened her jolly face, but not on the day of our parting; she was solemn and on the verge of tears. We didn't know if we would ever see each other again. It was a day we would never forget. I saw her standing with her mother at the Berlin train station, waiting for me, and *Mutti.* Our mothers, elegantly dressed in conservative well-tailored dark wool suits, didn't look conspicuous with their gray fox wraps draped nonchalantly over their shoulders. I was fascinated by the way the poor dead animal was worn. The entire skin of the fox was used, from head to tail. To keep the pelt from moving off the shoulder, one little leg was clipped to its mouth, like a clothespin on a wash line. It was bizarre. Sometimes I fantasized that the animal would come alive, jump off my mother's shoulder and scurry down the street . . . to freedom. Our mothers wore leather shoes with sensible heels, long gloves, and slouch felt hats like Marlene Dietrich. This was the style of the affluent woman of the 1930s . . . almost a uniform.

Our plan to leave Germany had to remain secret. Any leak to the Nazi's could have endangered our lives. Since I was an inquisitive and talkative child, my parents feared that I might inadvertently speak and be overheard. I was not aware of our plans until a week before our departure when crates suddenly appeared in our living room. It was then that my parents told me that we must leave Germany and move to America because of Hitler.

I was stunned. I was numb. I questioned myself: *How will we live there? What will I do? I don't know English . . . how will people understand me? I'll feel stupid in school. And what about Ruthchen? When will I see her again? What should I put in the crate? Certainly not my dolls . . . I'm getting too old for them. What do I leave behind . . . my best friend, Ruthchen?*

Heini, my fifteen-year-old brother, was different. He was quiet and introspective, and had known of the family's plans for weeks. My brother was treated like an adult and I . . . like the baby. Secrets . . . secrets . . . secrets. I couldn't tell Ruthchen, or look her straight in the eye. This was the reality for Jews in Germany in 1938.

For our departure my parents decided to separate our family for security reasons. My father and brother were scheduled to follow my mother and me by train a week after we were to leave. That frightened me. I wanted all of us to travel together . . . to stay as a family. I thought, *What if my mother and I got lost?* I wanted to be with my father. He could always make me smile. *Or what if something happened to my father and brother? What would my mother and I do?* A month ago we had heard that German troops had marched into Austria and had taken over the country "peacefully." It was called *Der Anschluss* (the takeover). On everyone's mind was, *"What's next?"*

The plan was to travel to Belgium, meet and stay with relatives in Antwerp and Brussels for six weeks while waiting for our U.S. visas, and then continue on to Paris for a week. The land journey would end in Le Havre, where we were to set sail on the beautiful *Normandie* to New York. In order for it to appear that we were on holiday, my father bought round trip train tickets to Belgium and France.

My parents were born in Austria-Hungary, which became Poland after WWI. They never wanted to become German citizens; and therefore my parents, Heini, and I had Polish documents, (although Heini and I were born in Berlin.) In April 1938, it was easier for Jews to leave Germany with a Polish passport. That law changed a few months later.

This was startling information for a ten-year-old to comprehend and certainly was difficult to keep secret from my best friend. I begged my parents to permit me to tell Ruth and for us to say our good-bye at the train station. Reluctantly, they agreed. Both Ruth and I were instructed to make no fuss. In those years it was not uncommon to see groups of people saying *adieu* at train stations, bearing bouquets of flowers and boxes of chocolates.

This day was not the right time for such loving displays. We had to be inconspicuous. It was an ordeal for young children to be unobtrusive while saying *Auf Wiedersehen* under such circumstances.

At the train station Ruth and I kept looking at each other for hidden messages. Out of fear we hardly spoke. Suddenly, I looked up from the platform and saw the billowing smoke of the approaching train. I can still conjure the smell of the steam from the massive engines and remember the dreaded good-byes. I squeezed my eyes shut, hoping that when I opened them there would be no train. It didn't work . . . time did not stand still. The train came to a grinding, screeching halt. The sound was profound. Whenever I see WW II films, I'm immediately transported to the Berlin train station and my Ruthchen.

Our mothers said *Auf Wiedersehen* to each other, formally shook hands, but affectionately kissed each of us. I felt a deep frustration, a tremendous urge to say something loving to Ruth's mother, but found it impossible. I was frightened. We were nervous, but careful to control our emotion, not to fidget, and not to commit a misdeed. I didn't want to make a mistake . . . I didn't want the Nazis to take us away. Ruth and I reluctantly hugged and looked deeply into each other's eyes; then with unspoken words, we parted. It was awful.

The sound of the train conductor's whistle was deafening. He kept looking at his gold watch. The dangling chain secured to his vest pocket mesmerized me. I fantasized that the chain would break and we'd all go home again. I awoke from my reverie as the conductor beckoned us to step onto the train. The steps suddenly seemed steep, endless, and unwelcome.

At that instant, I knew that an important chapter of our lives was ending. My mother lowered the window of our compartment. I leaned out as far as I could without losing my balance . . . trying to reach Ruth's upheld hand. Our arms were too short . . . we couldn't touch. I boosted myself out a bit more to get as close as possible to her. We broke our silence and she whispered, "I will write to you often." With tears running down our faces, Ruth and I simultaneously said, "I love you. I will miss you. Write soon."

With all our hearts we made that promise. How we controlled ourselves is incomprehensible to me now. Our hope was that Ruth's family would receive their visas to the United States quickly, and then we would all "live happily ever after," in New York, and continue our lives as before.

THERE'S A WITCH IN MY ROOM

There was a witch in my room! Where did she come from? She was scary. Who was she? . . . My goodness! . . . What was I to do? . . . I couldn't believe it . . . A WITCH . . . she was my Oma . . . Help! . . . Help! . . . I needed help . . . to get rid of MY OWN GRANDMOTHER!

The little old lady was ugly . . . really ugly. A large, raised dark birthmark above her lip sprouted coarse black hairs. They were stiff . . . like Brillo. My mother demanded that I kiss Oma goodnight . . . every night. And every night her kiss scratched me. I thought about pulling those hairs out . . . every last one of them . . . I'll get tweezers . . . or better still . . . not kiss her at all. No . . . I couldn't do that. My mother would be furious with me, and yet, I didn't see my parents or brother kiss Oma. *Why me? Always me? It's not my fault that I am only eleven years old, the youngest in the family. No one wants to hear what I think . . . don't I count?*

Oma's dark brown unflattering *sheitel* capped her head. *Sheitels* are wigs made of real hair that ultra-orthodox married Jewish women wear to make themselves unattractive to men. It sure worked on her! I wondered why, my tall, handsome, red-bearded, blue-eyed Opa married the witch? He surely didn't have to worry that other men might kidnap her . . . that's how ugly I thought she was.

It wasn't only her face and hair that was grotesque . . . her whole body looked repulsive to me. Her distended belly made her look pregnant. An old woman . . . pregnant! That was a disgusting thought for an eleven year old to contemplate. It embarrassed me. To complete the picture . . . she smelled horrible. Her breath reeked of leftover food, and her false teeth clicked when she ate. I hated it. Topping it off, her clothing smelled icky. I didn't want to be near her. That's how I remember Oma when I was eleven . . . not a pretty picture.

In 1934 when I was seven years old, and living in Berlin, Oma didn't look so awful to me. But what did I know? I was so young. She and Opa lived in a large apartment house, built circa 1850s, with rococo architecture, gargoyles framing the windows and lintels. The building's entrance had a high ornate archway that led to a central courtyard with a fountain. The feature that fascinated me the most was the naked cherubs looking toward the pool of water below. I was beguiled.

On some visits to my grandparents' house, I was lucky to see the performance of an organ grinder and his squealing monkey. The animal wore a little white shirt, bow tie, black jacket and short pants, topped by a fez. Is that where the expression *monkey suit came from?* To the animal's delight, people threw coins wrapped in pieces of newspaper from the windows of the five-story walk-up building. The monkey tipped his hat to his audience as he quickly picked up the coins. In a flash the organ grinder retrieved the money and put it into his own pocket. The louder the monkey chattered, the more money cascaded out of the windows.

Oma and Opa's home had many rooms with dark carved furniture, and massive wooden doors. My favorite was the dining room where the family gathered. On the credenza and tables, at any time of the day, there were bowls of fresh fruit, nuts, macaroons, rock candy, and sometimes, chocolates. My cousins took turns using the nutcracker . . . it was fun to hear the sounds the shells made when they snapped. It made a mess, but who cared? We kids happily cleaned it all up with that contraption with the soft brush we called *the silent butler*.

Above the center of the round table was a large chandelier with an enormous silk shade of embroidered heavy satin roses. The variations of colors went from neutrals to bright claret. The deep reds and burnished-gold braided tassels danced when a breeze came through the large open windows.

The movements of the colorful ornament made me think of gypsies dancing in the streets. I loved watching the bright, dark-eyed women squatting on the curb . . . their legs spread apart but covered by opulent long velvet dirndl skirts, low cut blouses exposing their cleavages . . . lots of gold jewelry, multiple jangling bracelets and the ubiquitous enormously shiny, gold hoop earrings. The gypsy earrings were the perfect embellishment for their beautiful, thick, dark, long hair. In warm weather their children wore no underpants, and from what I observed . . . and I looked . . . I don't think the women did either. Looking at these kids intrigued me . . . they were half naked . . . with bare bottoms! It was my first lesson in biology . . . I became aware of the difference in the sexes.

My mother didn't trust gypsies, believing they were thieves. I thought they were colorful . . . free as butterflies . . . unlike me.

Of Oma's six siblings, three sisters and a brother lived in the same apartment building as she. All were married and had children. I enjoyed visiting my grandparents, because I knew there would always be cousins to play with and Oma's house smelled of delicious cooking and baking.

Without question the large extended family went to my grandparents' house for all holidays. For Purim, one of my aunts wrote a play in which the children participated, while another sewed costumes, and an uncle magically produced props. The young children, boys and girls alike adored wearing outlandish makeup and garish clothes. What could be more exciting for little girls than to wear bright lipstick like the gypsies? Purim, the holiday of Queen Esther, was a joyous celebration with singing, dancing, drama, and of course, delicious food.

Passover, on the other hand, was a serious celebration. At the Seder, which began after sunset, we all sat around the huge dining table. The young children had to be extremely patient since the first part of reading the *Hagaddah* took at least an hour. Not until every word was recited were we permitted to eat . . . not even a morsel of matzo. The wait for the luscious chicken soup with the floating matzo balls was excruciating. It was not unusual to see several children asleep with their sweet heads (in the soup?) on the dining table. The adults were amused.

Two of Oma's sisters were interesting characters. The youngest married a poor scholar. It was an honor to marry an academic, even if he were penniless. The families pooled their resources and contributed to the household. This sister had three young children and struggled financially. I remember going to her apartment where I saw a sight I'll never forget: a dozen chickens and a few ducks, running around in the living room . . . squealing! Some women sat at the dining table, their wide skirts accommodating their spread-apart legs, as they plucked the poultry feathers into their laps. In the kitchen was the *shochet,* who according to Jewish law slaughtered the poultry in the most merciful way. The remaining screeching, lively inventory ran around the room. A few women stayed for hours, gossiping and perhaps starting their own juicy rumors. The sight was a child's fantasy . . . feather flying everywhere . . . it looked like a giant snow-globe. Nothing was wasted. The feathers were used to stuff pillows and quilts.

It was no secret that Oma's oldest sister was rich. She was tall and robust with a round pleasant face and rosy cheeks. Truthfully, she looked like a giant next to her short, hunch-shouldered, ashen-faced husband. He was the successful businessman, but at home, she was the boss.

No one liked her, not because they were envious of her wealth, but because she was stingy. A story repeated through the years went like this: Several relatives were invited to her home. She held one red apple in each hand, shined them up, one at a time, rubbing them ceremoniously on her Rubinesque backside. Then she offered them to her guests by divulging the price of each. "Eat, eat, they cost thirty *groshen*." We all went to Oma's house instead.

Food was important in our family. My grandparents hosted my brother's bar mitzvah at their house. It lasted from Friday night through Sunday. Henry was my parents' first-born child, a male, marking him special according to custom. In the Jewish orthodox religion male superiority was a practice I disapproved of, even before I became a teenager. I found the laws archaic and rigid. It caused friction between my parents and me.

Oma's sisters and maids cooked and baked for days before the festivities. All of the furniture in the dining room and the adjacent parlor were removed. The French doors were opened, and rows of tables were joined from room to room. White damask tablecloths were a beautiful setting for the china, silverware, crystal and the candle-lit silver candelabra. Dozens of relatives and friends were invited to Oma and Opa's home for lunch and dinner, after the synagogue services. A special table was set for the poor. I liked the fact that as a young child I was taught that it is a *mitzvah* to share good fortune.

At the temple, after Friday evening and Saturday morning services, braided chalah, schnapps, wine, herring, honey cake, nuts and dried fruits were provided for the entire congregation.

One of my fondest memories was at Oma's house, several days before the event. My mother took me along . . . to help plan for the bar mitzvah festivities. I needed to go to the bathroom. To my amazement the claw-footed bathtub was filled with live carp! There were so many . . . the poor fish struggled to swim. The floor was wet from the fish splashing furiously . . . struggling for air. It was the funniest thing I'd ever seen in my seven years. Their gymnastics fascinated me. I stuck my finger into their gaping mouths. It didn't hurt . . . actually I liked the sensation. Did the fish look at me as I smiled at them? Too bad none of my cousins were there to bear witness. Reality returned, and I remembered why I came to the bathroom, and made my exit with a smirk on my face.

My mother taught me to embroider when I was only a toddler. She boasted that at three, I was able to use scissors and thread a needle. The turning point of my handiwork came when at six, Oma taught me to crochet and knit. When my grandmother noticed my skills at such a young age, she also taught me to sew on the treadle sewing machine. It took some gymnastics and lots of energy to pump the pedal with my short legs, but it was worth it. Nothing was more magical than what I accomplished on that noisy contraption. I LOVED that machine.

Pieces of fabric magically appeared from Oma. She showed me how to make something, out of nothing. It triggered my love affair with clothing.

When I sewed clothes for my dolls, I felt powerful. Grandmother was instrumental in my becoming a fashion designer.

These were wonderful events that I remember doing with Oma when I was very young, living in Berlin . . . until April 1938.

After that spring, my family's pleasant life changed rapidly. To my amazement . . . one day . . . out of nowhere . . . empty boxes and cartons of all sizes suddenly appeared in the living room. I had to pack . . . quickly . . . we were moving to America in THREE DAYS! . . . AMERICA!

New York City, August 1939 (a year after arriving in America)

Without knocking, my mother entered my bedroom, and announced with much enthusiasm, "I have good news! Oma is coming to New York." I was absorbed reading Theodore Dreiser's *Jennie Gerhardt* and was caught off guard.

"Didn't you hear what I said?" my mother asked. She was annoyed . . . I hadn't paid attention.

"That's wonderful. When?"

"We just received news that Uncle Joe, his family and Oma left by ship from Le Havre yesterday. We've been anxious for news from them for over a year." I knew that the situation was scary. We hoped that they could get out of Germany in time.

Mother was nervous, and continued talking.

"They're getting out just in time . . . it might be the last ship to reach New York." (WW II was declared two weeks later, September 1939.) News reports on the radio proved her right. I just nodded in agreement. Becoming involved with *Jennie Gerhardt's* love life was more interesting. My mother didn't know that I was reading an adult book. The librarian had put it into my book-bag by mistake.

Suddenly I came out of my dream life. My mother was softly crying . . . she took a hankie out of her dress pocket, and blew her nose. I'd never seen her in such a state. When I looked at her she seemed embarrassed. Her voice sounded worried . . . anxious . . . and happy. I was confused.

"*Mutti,* that's wonderful," I finally said. I sat cross-legged on my bed, put my book down and fondled my soft pillow. "Where are they going to live?"

"Uncle Josef and his family are going to Bridgeport, where Uncle Morris found a house for them."

"That's good . . . and Oma? Is she going to live with Uncle Morris or Uncle Josef?"

"No. No. She's not going to them. Oma is going to stay with us." I heard her take a deep breath . . . it sounded painful. "She's going to be here," I heard my mother say in a sorrowful voice.

"Here? . . . Where?" I was stunned, and clutched the pillow hard against my flat chest.

"In our apartment, of course. I don't want to hear another word from you," she emphasized. *Did she read my mind?*

"What do you mean . . . in our apartment?" I said in amazement. My hands nervously played with my long, dark, curly hair. "We only have two bedrooms. You and Papa have one, I have the other, and Henry sleeps on the couch in the living room. I feel sorry for him . . . he has no privacy . . . that's not great . . . we don't have room for Oma." I was puzzled at my gut reaction. I had a premonition . . . a bomb was about to explode.

"Oma will sleep in your bedroom." She straightened her posture and put her crumpled handkerchief back into her pocket. Her grey-green eyes turned acid green. She glared at me. "You don't have to tell me where everyone sleeps in my own house." My mother looked like a cat . . . about to pounce.

"NO!" I exploded. "I don't want her in MY room." I threw my pillow down, jumped to the floor and stamped my feet, like a two-year-old. I had never had temper tantrums in my life and was embarrassed by my actions, but couldn't stop . . . I was out of control. What happened to the well-behaved child I was known to be? My outburst surprised even me, but I couldn't restrain my feelings. The most important place in the whole world was my room . . . my sanctuary . . . where I could fantasize . . . and keep the rest of the world out. *No one understands me.*

My mother scowled. "You ungrateful child. How can you be so heartless? This is your grandmother. You loved that she taught you to knit and sew when you were a little girl. Is this really you . . . so selfish? I can't believe your behavior. You won't give up just a part of your bedroom for your grandmother?" She was screaming now, waving her arms in no particular direction. "Aren't you ashamed?"

Part of me was.

"Why can't she move to Bridgeport, to Uncle Morris or Uncle Josef? They have big houses . . . with lots of rooms." That seemed reasonable to me.

When tears welled up, I opened my dresser drawer, fumbled for a hankie, and dabbed my eyes. I felt guilty . . . but at the same time I didn't want to share my room with an old lady, even if she WAS my grandmother!

"I'm only eleven-years-old," I cried, feeling sorry for myself, and playing baby. "I don't want an eighty-year-old in my bed."

"You unappreciative girl! I always thought you were smart. Have you suddenly become stupid, or what? Can't you figure it out? She's not going to be IN YOUR bed. We'll rearrange the furniture. Oma will have her own bed," my exasperated mother tried to explain.

"But my desk . . . I need my desk . . . and my lamp . . . to do my homework . . . and my dresser . . ." I babbled.

19

"You will share the dresser with Oma. I don't want to hear another word out of you. You should be happy that Oma was saved from Hitler. I will not mention this again. Subject closed."

She walked to the door and was about to leave, then stopped . . . turned toward me and said, "Wait until I tell your Papa about his favorite child. He'll be shocked. I'm ashamed that you're my daughter. He will feel the same," she was wailing. "I see it now . . . some day when I am old . . . you'll want to throw me out too!"

With that dramatic statement she whirled around, stormed out of my room, and slammed the door behind her. I was shattered. My mother had never done that before. But I learned something important . . . *I'm my* father's *favorite child.*

I heard her say that. She must have been angry to make such a statement. In my family everything is always a secret. On occasion, I've imagined that if my parents divorced, I'd go to my father. Now I was certain about that.

Curled up in my bed I cried and thought . . . *am I really a bad person? I guess I'm selfish . . . but I don't want Oma sleeping in my room. Why me?* I sobbed as I tossed on my bed, and beat my fist into the mattress with all my strength. *I'm glad that Hitler didn't kill Oma. I don't wish her any harm . . . what's the matter with Mutti . . . she's smart . . . why didn't she find another place for Oma to live in America? I don't want her in MY room . . . and that's the truth.* I was exhausted and fell into a fitful sleep.

Things were never the same again after Oma moved into not just my room, but also our home. She turned out to be a witch. How could she have changed so much in such a short time? It was less than two years since I last saw her in Berlin. What happened? I was puzzled . . . and miserable.

Of course there was no way out. I had to share my room with my octogenarian grandmother. It was awful from the start. I had no say in the matter. Although I understood what my mother told me, I didn't like anything about the arrangement. I tried to make the best of it . . . it wasn't easy. How could I accept all these changes so quickly? I was not yet twelve, and soon, a teenager. It was hard to take. They were going to take my room away . . . and with it . . . my privacy.

Furniture was moved to accommodate Oma's bed. Luckily I was able to keep my big desk. After school I spent much of my time in my room doing homework and listening to the radio. My favorites programs were *Mister Keene; Tracer of Lost Person, The Quiz Kids,* and the big band sounds of Glenn Miller, Benny Goodman, Artie Shaw, and a young Frank Sinatra.

I had to share my dresser with Oma. That was awful . . . her clothes smelled. But the worst part was at night when she took off her *sheitel* and put it on some wooden stand on top of my dresser that we now shared. It looked spooky, like some ghost leering at me when the light from the street

21

lamp made shadows on this creepy thing in my room. I wasn't scared, but I hated it.

Underneath the wig, Oma's head was shaved. I didn't want to look at her. Sometimes she put a scarf on her head . . . it was no improvement. But that's not all . . . she took her teeth . . . ALL of them . . . out of her mouth and put them into a glass of water on MY dresser . . . every night. Horrors! The first time I saw that, I gagged and almost threw up. When she was toothless and talked, I didn't understand a word. I tried to ignore her . . . the witch. We didn't talk to each other much. She spoke to me in German and I wanted to be an American . . . no German, if I could help it. I pretended that she was invisible . . . that wasn't easy . . . our apartment was small . . . she was always around.

Throughout this trauma, I had to be sweet and respectful. But how could I do that when she came into my room in the middle of the night, while I slept, and announced in her daytime voice, "Helgush, are you sleeping yet?" Even when I was still awake, I pretended otherwise. She woke me many times by putting on the light, opening the dresser drawers, one after another and making a racket. What was she looking for at those weird hours? Did she forget that I was just a kid . . . in the room we shared . . . and I had to get up early to get to school? How selfish of her.

Our phone was on a telephone table in the foyer. Oma sat in her big wing chair in the living room where she could see me, and hear my conversations. Since phones didn't have long cords there was no place to have private conversations. However, there were other places she could have sat . . . the kitchen . . . or OUR room, but of course she didn't chose to do that. When I was home, she always heard the phone ring, and sometimes answered it. My friends informed me that when they called and I wasn't home, they left messages. I never received them. Reluctantly I approached Oma. She claimed nobody called, and that my friends were liars.

Oma never made any friends during the five years she lived with us. We were all she had. It was suffocating. Many of my friends stopped coming to my house because they felt uncomfortable . . . and I understood. The witch followed us from room to room . . . always watching. I settled the situation by going to my friends' houses . . . sometimes sleeping over on weekends. How I wished that my parents didn't have European accents. I was embarrassed that mine weren't Americans born. By this time, I no longer had a trace of an accent. When I made new acquaintances, they all presumed I was like them . . . American born. I loved that.

Oma was also a tattletale. What happened to the nice Oma who taught me to knit, crochet and sew on the beloved treadle sewing machine when we lived in Berlin? This was not the same person.

In the five awful years that Oma lived in my room, she never gave me, or my brother, a birthday or Chanukka present. It wasn't a matter of finances . . . she wasn't poor.

Arrangements to transfer her money from Germany to the US had been made by my Uncle Morris years before her arrival in the States.

When she visited her two sons in Connecticut, she had lots of gifts to give her two daughters-in-law and four grandchildren, my cousins. They also found her to be cold, not the warm cuddly grandmother we used to know in Berlin. The gifts made me angry because my brother and I never got any (they probably would have been awful). And . . . she lived in my room . . . could you get any closer than that?

On these trips to her sons, I always wished she'd stay forever . . . for me to never see her again. That was a fantasy. Since my two aunts hated her, I knew Oma would return to my bedroom within a week. I saw no way out.

If only I could come into my room one day and find her dead. No . . . I don't mean that . . . I didn't want that to happen . . . I would be the one to discover her . . . a dead body in my room . . . oh, NO!

Why did my two aunts hate Oma? They had good reasons. Uncle Josef fell in love with his first cousin, Frida, Oma's niece. Grandmother didn't like her in the first place. Many nasty stories went back and forth. Words flew. There was constant bickering. Frida was the daughter of Oma's rich sister . . . the stingy one . . . remember the red apple episode? Oma was adamant: her first-born son was NOT going to marry his first cousin. But Frida and Uncle Josef did marry. Oma stopped talking to her daughter-in-law but stayed in touch with her adoring first-born son. Can you blame Aunt Frida for not wanting her angry mother-in-law to live in her house in America?

The other daughter-in-law was Aunt Sophie. Why was she against Oma living with her in America? Oma's second son fell in love with Sophie, when she was in her teens . . . he about ten years her senior. She was a blond, blue-eyed beauty, with a dazzling dimpled smile.

The time was Austria-Hungary, 1913. Uncle Morris left for America at twenty-one to seek his fortune. If he stayed in Europe he would have had to fight in WW I. My uncle was not the typical Jewish immigrant. The majority of Eastern Europeans settled in the Lower East Side of Manhattan. Morris met a passenger on the four-week voyage to New York. His new acquaintance suggested that my uncle settle in Salt Lake City, Utah, where there were more opportunities for young, unattached men. It was good advice. Not having an occupation, Morris became a peddler. He went from house to house, selling household wares right out of his suitcases. Within five years, this frugal, ambitious young man, invested his hard-earned money in Utah's silver mines. My uncle became prosperous. After the war, he returned to the *shtetl* to visit his family, but especially to see sweet Sophie. She was the beauty he remembered, and she stole his heart all over again.

However, their romance became complicated. They had two problems: First: Max Reinhardt, a well-known producer and director of early films was visiting their hometown. By chance he saw Sophie and was dazzled by her ravishing looks. Reinhardt tried to persuade her to come to Vienna, the movie capital of Europe, and promised to put her in his films. Uncle Morris was shocked by the news. In a fit he exclaimed:

"No movies, Sophie! I don't want you to be an actress. We'll get married and I'll take you to Brooklyn, America!"

Second: Oma was vehemently against the match. She believed that Sophie, from a poor family, was a gold digger. My grandmother thought that the marriage was Sophie's escape to get out of the small town . . . with her rich son. The couple was in love. Just the sight of this beautiful young woman would make any man's heart melt. Oma said, "Definitely NOT!" Morris said, "Absolutely, YES!" They got married and moved to Brooklyn, New York.

It's no wonder Oma was not welcomed to live in Sophie's house in America. When Oma visited her son's families, she never stayed long. Nobody liked her. My relatives felt sorry for me, but that was of no help . . . I was stuck with my grandmother.

My mother was stuck with Oma, too. What did my father and brother think? I never heard the subject discussed. All was quiet. Well, not really. Mutti and Oma argued all the time. Their confrontations made me uncomfortable, but at least I wasn't the only one who had problems. My brother never said a word. I wanted to escape . . . but at my age . . . where would I go . . . what were my options?

One day my mother became furious with my grandmother. Oma wanted to keep busy and volunteered to go to the live chicken market, a few blocks from our house.

Mutti agreed and gave her an extra ten cents to have the chicken-flicker clean the fowl completely. It was winter; my grandmother wore a navy blue wool coat, gloves and scarf. The market was a great place to socialize and hear all the gossip. Oma came home several hours later, carrying a warm, freshly killed chicken. Feathers were stuck all over her coat and she trailed oodles more behind her when she walked into the house. Oma didn't pluck the chicken to save the money, but because it gave her something to do. When my mother saw her with all the feathers, she screamed at Oma. I thought the scene humorous, but I carefully kept a straight face.

My mother made a surprise Sweet Sixteen party for me. It was the American thing to do, and she wanted to please me. I wish it had never happened. The party was the most boring, dreadful gathering I ever attended . . . and it was my very own! It was 1943 . . . there were no boys in their late teens available for me to date . . . it was WWII . . . they were in uniform . . . mostly overseas. Boys my age didn't interest me. Actually, it's a good thing that there were none, since my party was so awful. I would have been mortified.

At the party, Oma sat in the huge wing chair. She looked absurd with her short legs and clunky brown oxford shoes dangling, like a small child not being able to touch the parquet floor. To complete the fashion description, she wore her ugly wig and an awful dark dress that would have been more appropriate for a funeral . . . not her granddaughter's birthday party.

She was the overseer. I think it would have pleased her to point her short pudgy fingers at us, if we had transgressed. It drove me crazy. The witch sat there . . . watching . . . watching . . . watching. My mother was no better; she also acted like the Gestapo. What did they think we girls were going to do? How would they have acted if there had been boys at the party? I wanted to get out of there; but how could I? I was the guest of honor!

Even the nut cake my mother baked for the occasion was a disaster. That wasn't an appropriate cake for a Sweet Sixteen party . . . and besides . . . there were shells in it. One of my friends could have choked to death! This was MY birthday, not a celebration for some fifty-year old lady from Europe. Who in their right mind serves a nut cake with shells for a Sweet Sixteen birthday party?

I would have loved a cake from a bakery with red roses and chocolate frosting. For goodness sakes, doesn't my mother understand anything . . . this is AMERICA! But, of course, I never said anything.

P.S. No birthday present from Oma.

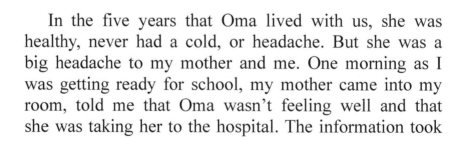

In the five years that Oma lived with us, she was healthy, never had a cold, or headache. But she was a big headache to my mother and me. One morning as I was getting ready for school, my mother came into my room, told me that Oma wasn't feeling well and that she was taking her to the hospital. The information took me by surprise. Automatically I kissed my grandmother good-bye, and wished her good luck. I was so aware of my true feelings . . . guilt . . . and all that went with it.

"Helgush, I am not coming back." she said. She was correct. Oma died the following day.

Her funeral was the first I attended. It seemed surreal. I didn't cry. I felt that Oma didn't like me . . . I didn't like her. How I ached for an affectionate grandmother like many of my girlfriends had.

P.S. I got my bedroom back.

Twenty years after my grandmother died, Aunt Sophie revealed a startling epic about her mother-in-law, my Oma. We were sitting in Sophie's cozy den, having a cup of coffee and nibbling on her freshly baked apple-strudel, when I expressed how sad it was that no one liked Oma, the last five years of her life in America. I emphasized how uncaring she had been to all of us. It was then that Aunt Sophie unfolded the saga:

Oma, was born in Tarnow, in Austria-Hungary in the mid-1800s. She married a handsome redheaded, bearded man, a scholar, well respected in the community. They had five children. Opa sold books, but it was Oma who supported the family. She had a cottage industry, making wigs for orthodox Jewish women. Grandmother employed several workers. Her business was successful. When she heard that in New York City her venture might flourish, she became intrigued and seriously looked into the prospect of traveling across the ocean. How did one get accurate information in 1905?

Oma was going to New York City. She made arrangements for the care of her five young children, one not yet of school age. Although Opa, was a scholar and earned money teaching, it was Oma's cottage industry manufacturing wigs that provided the main family income. Opa became the temporary manager. Obviously there was sufficient money and household help for her to make such a daunting trip to the New World. With her astute business sense and thorough preparation, her business enterprise continued while she was away. The voyage from Hamburg, Germany, to Ellis Island, took six weeks. My grandmother temporarily moved to the Lower East Side of Manhattan.

In less than a year, she again endured the six week Atlantic crossing back to Tarnow. Grandmother had much to report to her family and friends on her return. Oma stated that the living conditions on the Lower East Side were horrible. The buildings were five and six story walkups, with one toilet on each floor. Many apartments had perhaps twenty, or more people sharing one toilet. The bathtub was in the kitchen. The streets were congested, noisy, day and night. Much of life transpired there. Hygiene was low and disease high. Oma saw how unsatisfying the situation was. When she returned home, she said that with trees and flowers, Tarnow was more sanitary, healthier and more beautiful than the little bit she saw of America. As for her business expectations . . . they were probably overblown.

I was stunned by the story. What was in her satchels on her return home? Did she have presents for her children? What were they? Was she happy to see her husband Jacob?

How I crave this knowledge . . . but time has run out . . . it is too late. There is no one alive who has that information.

My grandmother's incredibly brave excursion did not leave my thoughts. Did Oma run away? She was a young married woman, perhaps in her mid-late-twenties, in 1905. It took guts for her to leave her husband, five young children and make such a daunting voyage. Had it been her intention to leave the small town and make a life for herself in America? Perhaps she was a feminist before we knew the meaning of the word. I try to imagine her, this petite vigorous woman, with her satchels on board the large, crowded ship, all by herself. What was in those valises? Were they of leather with many straps or heavy brocaded fabric? I visualize Oma wearing a white high collared long sleeved blouse, long full, black skirt, and high buttoned dark brown leather shoes. She must have been strong to carry heavy luggage . . . one in each hand?

At the beginning of the 20th Century the passengers making this odious trip were mostly males, single, married, and some with families. Was she the only married female aboard who was traveling by herself? Was she attractive to the men? Did they flirt? Did she? Did she acknowledge her marital status, if asked? Crossing from New York, back to Hamburg took forty-five days. Did they encounter storms on the open Atlantic? Did she make friends on the long journey? Did she get seasick? Did anyone help her, if she had?

Oma obviously had tremendous self-confidence. Was it her intention to leave her family and start a new life away from Tarnow? Or perhaps she was subconsciously seeking romance. Was she maternal?

She returned to her family and admitted that the journey was for naught. Grandmother just picked up the pieces and continued her life as before.

Is that how it was? . . . I can only speculate.

———

Another aspect of Oma's life was revealed to me the night of my mother's funeral, twenty-six years after Oma died.

I decided to sleep in my parents' house that evening and keep my father company. My parents had been married fifty-two years. The night of the burial was the first time my father and I, were together as adults. That was an extraordinary milestone.

Papa, who was not talkative, opened up his heart to me. He talked about having been born in the same town as my mother. They had not yet met, although their families knew of each other. First he fell in love with a beautiful dark-eyed woman from his hometown. It was WWI, and he was a soldier in the Austrian-Hungary army. My father promised to marry her as soon as the war was over. Time passed . . . the war ended after four long years. He returned home, unscratched, and found his love. Papa repeated his vows to her, but his beloved refused him. He was devastated. With that realization he made an immediate decision to leave his country, relatives and friends. Papa moved to

Germany where there were many opportunities for young, bright men, than in Poland. (After WWII, Austria-Hungary became Poland.)

———

My father was given entrée to the Wolf family in Berlin, who had formally lived in his hometown. Papa presented himself, and was welcomed. The Wolfs had three sons, one lived in America; the other two lived in Berlin, with their parents, as did the unmarried daughter. My father obviously impressed the family as they continued to invite him to their home. At some point the Wolf family offered him financial help to go into business. (Did he ask, or did they make the offer?)

To show his gratitude, Papa started to "keep company" with their daughter. Hilda was beautiful, with strawberry blond hair, green cat-like eyes, tall, and carried herself regally. I perceive she was in her late-twenties and still single, (old in those years) because she was smart and extremely opinionated . . . a negative trait for women of that era.

My father married her.

He continued his story for hours. "I was not in love with your mother, but married her out of gratitude to her parents. They helped me become a successful businessman."

I was shocked and saddened by that revelation. It was traumatic to hear this admission. He continued talking about his life and admitted that he eventually fell in love with my mother. I think he was in awe and intimidated by her . . . but love? . . . I'm not sure.

Now I understand why my father kept quiet when Oma came to live with us. It was his way of re-paying his mother-in-law for the generous support she and Opa gave him when he was a young man. With their financial backing he was able to go into his own business and become a successful entrepreneur.

I see the picture of Oma's life differently, now that I'm her age. In Berlin she had a lovely spacious home where we all congregated, a loving husband, relatives and friends by her side. She was the revered matriarch.

When she came to the United States in 1939, she was a widow (Opa died a natural death in Berlin) no longer the dowager. Her youngest son immigrated to Johannesburg, South Africa in 1934. She never saw him again. Instead of having a loving spouse who was supportive of her whims, she had two daughters-in-law who disliked her. No longer did she have a home of her own. Instead she lived with her daughter's family and didn't even have a room of her own. Oma had to share a bedroom with her eleven-year old granddaughter, me, for the last five years of her life.

Now I understand her unhappiness. Leaving her comforts in Berlin at eighty to come to America probably didn't please her. But what choice did she have . . . dying under the Nazis . . . or dying of old age with her family by her side . . . in America?

During the last five years of her life, when she lived in my bedroom, Oma was not the kind, loving, supportive grandmother I knew when we lived in Berlin. Seven decades later I looked through old family albums and was shocked. There were many photos of my grandparents taken in Europe. I didn't need a magnifying glass to see that Oma had lovely features; arched thick eyebrows, big dark eyes, small nose and sensual lips. Except for the wig, she was actually pretty.

I, a visual artist, had been blind. How could I have been so myopic? Psychologically it proves that if you dislike someone intensely, it is difficult to be objective.

The life lessons she taught me when I was a young girl in Berlin, are still with me. The crocheting, knitting and particularly teaching me how to operate the treadle machine, gave me the desire and calling to become a fashion designer; an occupation I loved, my whole life. For that, I thank you, Oma.

I've come to the sad conclusion that Oma was depressed and melancholy all the years she lived in my bedroom, in America.

I'm sorry, Oma.

She died at eighty-six.

ACROSS THE STREET

"**I** feel sorry that Caroline is Catholic," I blurted out.

"Why? What's wrong with being Catholic? What difference does it make to you . . . the liberal? Anyway, we have no say-so. Religion is given to us when we're born," said my wise, thirteen year old friend.

"Well that's true. But I'm glad I'm not in Caroline's shoes."

". . . and why not?"

"You and I have it much easier than Catholics," I said emphatically.

"Oh, yeah? Explain that one. It's hard enough being a teenager, but what does religion have to do with it?"

"I admit, we work hard in school, do our homework and get good marks," I explained. "Our parents expect that. They're nervous right now . . . both of our brothers are in the service." It's 1942 . . . a scary year. "We only have a few household chores to do: keep our room neat, set the table, wash the dishes, throw out the garbage . . . and write letters to the soldiers and sailors overseas. That's really not asking too much. By comparison, we're lucky. We have weekends free to be with friends, go to the movies and sleepovers. But that's not the case with poor Caroline."

"What about poor Caroline?"

"Every Saturday, she and her three older sisters have to clean the whole house, do heavy laundry, wash floors, and everything else you can think of. They do spring cleaning every week!"

"Wow! But what does that have to do with being Catholic?" my friend asked again.

"Because you and I can sleep as long as we wish on Sundays," I said with a sigh of relief. "But Caroline has to be at church for the 6 a.m. Mass with her mother and sisters. Her father stays home. She has to get up by five . . . at dawn . . . for goodness sakes! Poor girl. And if that isn't enough . . . as soon as the women come home from church . . . they get busy cooking the Sunday Italian dinner. There could be a dozen or more people for the feast.

The women do all the cooking and cleaning while the men sit, eat and enjoy the afternoon. Do you understand now why I don't want to be a Catholic?"

Caroline lived directly across the street from my apartment in New York City. My family resided in the only new elevator building in the neighborhood, built in 1939. My bedroom windows faced her tenement. That's where the similarity ended. The brick dwelling in which she lived, erected in the mid-1800s, impressed me from the outside, with its bas-relief, gargoyles and large windows. But the inside showed anything but splendor. The six floor walk-up tenement had steep, creaky, wooden steps.

There were eight apartments on each floor. The hallways were dark and creepy at night. Most houses in the neighborhood were of this vintage. Caroline's building was renovated after the turn of the century with indoor plumbing, a toilet in each apartment, rather than one communal lavatory on each floor. After completion Caroline's house was considered "modern."

When entering the apartment you stepped directly into the kitchen. It was small but had a window, a bath/wash tub, stove, oven, a few cabinets, but no icebox. With no space in the kitchen and no foyer, the icebox ended up in the living room. The deliveryman had a horrendous job carrying the heavy blocks of ice, up the four steep flights of stairs. One of Caroline's chores was emptying the pan under the icebox of accumulated water. In order to save money, some neighbors placed milk and other perishables on the outside windowsills in the winter.

The deep, large washtub interested me . . . no . . . disturbed me. The family bathed in the kitchen. When not in use, the board on top of the tub became the work counter. Next to it was a shallow sink used for washing dishes, as well as for ablutions. A small table and a few chairs were squeezed into the tiny space. During the week the family ate in shifts. Caroline's mother served, but didn't eat until everyone had finished their meal. Since every member of the family came home at different times, from school and work, her mother was in the kitchen almost all day. The last one home received food that had been warmed up several times on top of the radiator. (Radiators provided steam heat several hours a day in the winter.)

The kitchen's narrow doorway led into the living room. From there one went through the first of three bedrooms . . . one into the next . . . a railroad flat . . . no doors or privacy. The girl's bedrooms were tiny, with one bed shared by two sisters, and a small dresser. None had closets, or windows, except the last bedroom which Caroline's parents occupied.

The tub presented a problem. Since the only entrance to the apartment was the kitchen, (that's where the tub was) schedules had to be made . . . who . . . and when . . . the five women and one man could take their baths. Under those conditions baths were not taken every day, and showers didn't exist. Caroline's oldest sibling was twenty-two, and the other two sisters were teenagers. Her father had a great excuse to play cards with his cronies in the neighborhood "social club" when the women bathed. We heard lots of juicy stories about what went on in the back rooms of the club.

Caroline and I walked eight blocks to junior high school every morning. Her looks fascinated me. She was not a beauty in the pure sense of the word; I found her exotic. Her long thick brown hair, framed her broad face, accentuating her large dark eyes, arched eyebrows and sensuous mouth. However, it was her Roman nose that intrigued me. The length and curve were beautiful, as if an artist had chiseled it. I found myself staring at her many times.

One day I received an invitation to Sunday dinner at her house. I was thrilled, but apprehensive. I had to check with my mother and knew the outcome in advance.

"You can't go. The food is not kosher."

I desperately wanted to go, but couldn't, and gave a lame excuse. Months later Caroline extended another invitation, but nothing had changed my mother's mind. It was embarrassing for me. We lived in a mixed neighborhood of Italians and Jews, who respected each other, but obviously didn't know the other's rituals. The invitations stopped coming.

After junior high school, Caroline and I went to different high schools and didn't see each other often. One day we met and invited me to Sunday dinner again. This time I accepted immediately, but kept the date a secret from my mother. She thought I was going to another girlfriend's house. I felt guilty. It was a momentous decision. At that point I realized I was growing up and gaining independence.

Caroline's Sunday Italian dinner transported me into imagining that I was a character in an Italian film. The living room seemed larger than I remembered. The grand oval table looked inviting with its colorful embroidered white cloth and napkins. The silverware gleamed and the sparkling wine goblets were rapidly filled, and refilled. I politely refused, but Caroline's father insisted. I smiled. I smiled a lot that afternoon . . . the people were so gracious and warm. My family was not like that . . . casual and fun.

I sized up the interior and noticed the heavily carved mahogany breakfront. Porcelain Madonnas, dried flowers in vases, and old family wedding pictures in silver frames were showcased. Heavy drapes with tasseled gold sashes framed the sheer curtained windows. The herringbone parquet floor was beautiful. A Persian throw rug was almost invisible under the dining table.

The conversations flowed. I loved the good-natured humor and laughter, but the food got most of my attention. It smelled divine. The women took turns going into the kitchen. First, a bowl of the largest steaming hot meatballs I have ever seen appeared. The aroma of tomatoes, garlic, cilantro and basil filled the air. I must have impressed Caroline's father with my appetite, since he immediately refilled my plate. I had never had meatballs solo, and thought it odd. What happened to the spaghetti? When the pasta came out, I thought that was the end of dinner. But no . . . it was just the beginning! Roasted chicken, gnocchi, stuffed artichoke, pork chops and olives followed. I could have made a meal of any of those foods that appeared from the magical kitchen. The wine kept flowing.

That dinner taught me a lesson for the next time . . . I will pace my appetite. Caroline's father constantly encouraged me to, "Eat. Eat." The dessert was an unforgettable, delicious, decadent, tiramisu. I fondly remember my first Italian Sunday dinner with Caroline's family. Years later I saw the whole picture and realized that for Caroline being Catholic and going to 6 a.m. Mass every Sunday was not a hardship.

I never told my mother about that glorious meal.

THE ANTIQUE GOLD WATCH

I loved my stepmother. I loved my father. My mother was another story . . . but not for today. Papa was a very kind, hardworking, affectionate, loving man. It was easy to read him by looking at his dark, twinkling eyes.

Frequently he was able to manipulate me with eye contact, which in essence said, "Do this for me, Helga, so that your mother won't be upset." I often disagreed with her and that was forever a bone of contention between us. Unfortunately, my mother was much stronger than Papa. She made all the rules. He adored her and at the same time feared her anger. In my parents' house my father was like Neville Chamberlain . . . "Peace at any price." I felt the price was too high. Although I loved him dearly, sometimes I thought him weak.

The day my mother died, I spent the night in my parents' house. My father talked for hours, into the early morning, about his life with her. I was fascinated and realized that this was probably the first time in fifty-two years that he was able to say whatever he felt, and without interruption. I cannot recollect ever having had a one-on-one conversation with him because my mother was always present, and in full command. It occurred to me that when he did make a statement, she usually negated what he said. The situation upset me. But Papa wanted peace.

I never heard my parents raise their voices. My mother felt that impolite. Years later I became aware that I did the same. When angry I spoke in a low modulated tone, looking the person straight in the eye . . . controlling. True emotions were locked up.

After my mother died, my father and I met for lunch once a week, in mid-town Manhattan, where I worked. New York City is known for its diverse and wonderful restaurants. For two years, until I moved to Miami, Florida, we went to the same kosher vegetarian restaurant that my father favored. It was important for us to be together, to talk, and get to know each other. And talk we did. He told me about the many ladies who wanted to go out with him. His sister-in-law, Frieda, pursued him. She was my mother's first cousin, who married my mother's oldest brother. My mother never liked Frieda as a cousin and liked her even less as a sister-in-law. This was the one and only time the whole family totally agreed with my mother.

Finally my father told me about Binnie. Both families knew each other casually for fifteen years. A friend suggested that he, the eligible and kind bachelor, take her out for coffee. The rest is history. They fell in love. Their ages added up to one hundred and fifty-four years; he, seventy-nine and she, seventy-five, when they married.

Shortly after the nuptials I moved to Miami. They, in turn, became "snow-birds" and rented a lovely apartment at a residential hotel in South Beach. The three of us usually had weekly dinners. It was always the highlight for me to see this wonderful elderly loving couple. Binnie was almost perfect except . . . she was not a good cook.

Neither I nor my father cared about that. She was a warm, outgoing, intelligent, affectionate person. Everyone loved her. I once told my father, in front of Binnie, that I wished SHE had been my biological mother!

We were eating dinner. It was the last evening, the end of the season, before my father and Binnie were going back to New York. I told my father if he ever wanted to give me a gift, I would love to have his gold pocket watch. He wore it for years when I was young but in the past years he kept it in the vault. I was especially attracted to its history. Papa told me that the indentations on the gold watch cover were from my baby teeth . . . it was my teething ring!

My father's response to my request was shocking. "If you go back to your husband, I will give you the watch."

I couldn't believe what he had said . . . this from my loving father. I was furious. This time I did not speak in a modulated tone. Suddenly my whole body reacted to my anger . . . I felt flushed . . . my head was throbbing. I looked deeply into my father's eyes and said, "You never asked me why I left Al. Do you think I would go back to a marriage I don't want to be in . . . for a gold watch?" My head was bursting . . . I was so angry . . . bewildered. What happened to the loving man? He sounded like my mother. Did she come back from the dead and enter my father's body? I was astonished.

The room became embarrassingly quiet. My father bowed his head in shame. Binnie was stunned. I was hyperventilating. What happened the rest of the evening? I don't remember.

November of the same year, my father and Binnie returned for the season. I was invited to dinner at their apartment. We kissed and hugged . . . so glad to see each other again after seven months. My father gently released himself from our embrace and handed a large shopping bag to me.

He watched as I took out the magnificent silver candelabra that had been in his parents' home in Austria-Hungary since the mid-1800s. It was my father's inheritance. The candelabra was in my parent's home in Germany and finally in the United States. Mine was a love-hate relationship with the magnificent antique because it was my chore to polish it every Thursday night for the Sabbath.

I was extremely touched by the gift. It was the only remnant from my father's childhood. When I casually peered into the shopping bag before folding it, and disposing of it, I discovered a small plain brown paper bag at the bottom. I lifted it out and before opening it; my father and I looked at each other . . . no conversation . . . our eyes spoke.

There was the gold watch!

He Kissed Him

He kissed him first! I was furious. I was confused. I was puzzled.

My father hadn't wanted me to marry Al. Actually, neither had my mother. Knowing the type of person she was, I knew that my mother put my father up to "talk to your daughter." That's how she manipulated us; when my mother couldn't get through to me, she used my father. Usually it succeeded. With his bright twinkling eyes, my father conveyed without words, "Helga, do this for me, or your mother will be impossible to live with."

It generally worked, but not this time. I wouldn't budge. I knew that Papa loved me, but I was tired of being used. Also, I was angry that he permitted my mother to always call the shots. Papa believed that was the road to peace in our family. Our home was always quiet . . . no one raised their voice . . . that was impolite. But deep down inside . . . was there peace?

Sheepishly (he looked uncomfortable not making his usual eye contact), my father uttered these words, "You marry Al . . . you make your own bed . . . you sleep in it."

That seemed good to me, but of course, that's not what he meant.

There was no changing my mind. I found the right man for me: intelligent, the right age, the right religion, hardworking, and in love with me. We both had good jobs and I knew we would do well in the future. My parents were concerned because he came from a poor and uneducated family.

I had had a summer romance with a dental student who lived in Springfield, Mass. He visited me several times in New York City. My parents liked him, probably because of his profession. It was clear to me that I didn't love him enough to give up my dream of being a fashion designer in New York. I could not imagine myself living in a small town, and not being near Greenwich Village.

Al was the one for me.

The entire wedding party, Al, me, the rabbi, my parents, mother-in-law, best man, maid and matron of honor, stood under the *chuppah*. Al and I had already shared the first sip of wine from the same beaker; the groom, as a symbol of good luck, broke the glass . . . the rabbi pronounced us man and wife . . . and then . . . my father stepped forward . . . grabbed Al . . . and kissed him!

What happened? Doesn't the bride get the first kiss? I was shocked.

The guests thought it amusing and laughed. I was shocked . . . confused. For a moment I stood under the wedding canopy in disbelief . . . all alone . . . abandoned. I felt stood up. Didn't I have a role in this ceremony?

What happened to my father? Was he suddenly happy that I got married? Was he glad to be rid of me? Was my newly-minted husband now acceptable to him?

After much soul searching I have come to the conclusion that my father was never actually against Al. He was just doing his job . . . agreeing with my mother . . . keeping the peace.

Peace . . . At what price?

Baba Lillie Becomes a US Citizen

She was old when I met her. Really not so old . . . perhaps fifty-three . . . but she looked ancient. Lehke was born on the second day of Passover, according to the Hebrew calendar. However, she wasn't certain of the year.

Her childhood had been difficult and puzzling. Puzzling, because she disliked talking about her past; it was too traumatic. Her parents died when she was very young. We never knew the circumstances. Maternal grandparents raised the four sisters, Lehke being the second oldest. It was the early 1900s, the time of pogroms in Russia against the Jews. Sometimes when pressed for more information, she said that Cossacks killed her parents. I felt she was witness or victim of horrific situations. The happenings remain secret.

Lehke claimed that she had had a stocking factory when she was eleven years old. I could not visualize such a young child being in her own business, but she was adamant about the statement. Throughout the years, when she repeated the claim, her posture became erect; she looked proud. Maybe it was true . . . but at eleven?

At this point of her young life, two of her sisters moved to America. The grandparents died, and Lehke became the mother to her youngest sister, who was only a toddler. Sometimes she said her business supported her; at other times she lamented that they starved. Her stories were inconsistent and difficult to put into proper prospective.

Life continued to be troublesome. She married Jacob, and gave birth to two children within two years. The political situation became intolerable in Russia before WWI. Her husband dreamed that in America he could make a better life for his family. He went to New York City. Jacob planned to send for his wife and children as soon as he earned enough money to book passage for them. The family name was Geweritz. When he landed on Ellis Island, an employee who couldn't pronounce it, suggested a "real" Jewish/ American Name:Horowitz.

Unfortunately WWI intervened. For eight years Lehke and the young children were left in Russia, under dire circumstances. The Cossacks invaded her town. She claimed the family survived on potatoes.

There was an exodus of Eastern European Jews to the United States. The majority settled in New York City. In many cases, it was married men who left their families behind for years, until they were financially able to bring them to America. Some started a new life in America and "forgot" about their relatives. These were difficult times . . . lack of education . . . no knowledge of English . . . working long hours . . . living in over-crowded conditions, and loneliness. For many life was miserable.

But Jacob remembered his responsibilities. In 1922 Lehke crossed the ocean with her two children. Her husband greeted his family at Ellis Island, and brought them to Reading, Pennsylvania, where he had an inn. Lehke talked lovingly of the beautiful dishes, pots, pans and linens that were waiting for her in their apartment, above the establishment. She enjoyed living in "the mansion." Her third child, Abie, the REAL American, was born within the year. To Lehke giving birth in a hospital was the American way. She considered herself modern.

Paradise didn't last long. Her husband's business partner was a gambler, lost all their money, and ran away. Reluctantly they moved to Brooklyn, N.Y. Jacob scraped money together and opened a fruit and vegetable store where Lehke helped out six days a week. Although she didn't know how to write, she was able to add numbers. Newspapers were used for wrapping the produce. They eked out a living. She was happy to be able to give her children fresh food.

Abie, eventually changed his name to Al. The American born child, excelled in school. Lehke Americanized her name to Lillie. Life was hard but better than in Russia. Al was in an accelerated class in high school. The family was proud of the young "Yankee."

Things were looking up, but not for long. Jacob got brain cancer and died. At sixteen the "Yankee" child graduated from high school with honors. Al was drafted into the Army and returned to Brooklyn when the war ended.

He entered Pratt Institute, on the GI Bill, to study engineering. I was studying fashion design at Pratt. We met, fell in love, and married. Lillie became my mother-in-law. When Al and I had children, they called their grandmother, Baba Lillie. She was frugal. For her birthday I bought her a sweater. She acknowledged the gift with, "I don't need it."

"Mom, how can you say that? Your cardigan has holes at the elbow."

To set me straight, she showed me three "brand new" sweaters, still in their original wrappings. Her sons had given them to her over the past ten years.

My children loved her. I wanted to do something special for my mother-in-law, and bought the best seats for "Fiddler on the Roof." The day following the performance I called to hear her reaction to the play. She hated it!

"Why?" I asked in disbelief.

"It made me suffer all over again, like I did in Russia. I want to see something happy," was her explanation. Her critique made me realize my error.

Through casual conversation, I learned that Baba Lillie was not an American citizen. "Mom, you've been in this country for more than thirty year. Your sons went to war to protect our nation. I know that you love America. Why aren't you a citizen?"

She admitted her reason; she was illiterate and feared failing the test.

I insisted. The family joined to help her pass the exam. All of us took turns studying with her. Baba Lillie found the process difficult. At times she became exasperated and on the verge of tears. She was fearful; she wanted to quit. We all supported her by saying, "You can do it!"

The most difficult part was teaching her to sign her name. Her eyeglasses fogged up; she was nervous. Finally she was ready. The important day arrived. My sister-in-law and I were her witnesses at court.

Baba Lillie kept wiping her brow and cleaning her fogged-up glasses.

We waited for her name to be called. Her turn came. She was asked several questions which she remembered well. The last question was, "Who was the first president of the United States?"

Her face lit up. She knew this one. With utmost confidence, loud and clear, she answered, "President Roosevelt!"

I looked at the judge's face. It was kind and amused. He helped her by saying, "You mean George Washington. Right?"

Baba Lillie quickly said, "Yes. Yes, Your Honor."

Everyone stood to recite the Pledge of Allegiance. I noticed my mother-in-law's face as she placed her right hand on her heart; her eyes filled with tears of joy. Baba Lillie wiped her fogged up eyeglasses one more time. With a pen in her shaking hand she slowly signed her name to the document.

Congratulations, Baba Lillie. You are an American Citizen!

She looked proud. And so were we.

THAT LETTER!

That letter! I read it again, and again.

Can it be so?

Are you really coming?

Really?

All of you?

Was I, am I, dreaming?

In January 1962, I received a letter from Ruth informing me that her husband Israel, a neurologist and psychiatrist, had been awarded a one-year fellowship to study the encephalograph machine at Mount Sinai Hospital, in New York City. He was the only doctor chosen from Chile to study that specialty. The decision for him to represent his country was a great honor. In time Israel would train others to do likewise.

This was thrilling news. He would be able to bring Ruth and their two children, Gaby, 13, and Arturo, 11, to stay in New York for one year. Ruth and I would finally be together again after twenty-four years. Our dream was coming true.

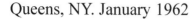

Queens, NY. January 1962

Dearest Ruthchen,

I'm so excited.
I can't wait.
Our dream is coming true!
I'm thrilled to be able to see you and to meet your family. Every day since I received the fabulous news I think about the wonderful experience this will be for all of us. Susie and Jeffrey looked at photos albums filled with pictures that you have sent me over the past twenty-four years. My children looked at the Atlas to see how far you will travel from Chile to New York City. It will be great for our families to get to know each other. We will learn new things . . . what fun we will have! I told the whole world that my best friend since we were five is coming to New York for a whole year. My parents are very anxious to see little Ruthchen again. I'm planning parties to introduce you to everyone.
I love you.
Soon, soon, we will hug each other again.
Love, and millions of kisses to all of you.
Have a marvelous flight.
Our dreams will become reality.

Love, Helga

Queens, NY. February 1962

Dearest Ruthchen,

I'm excited . . . I have good news. Right off beautiful Central Park I found a marvelous Apartment/Hotel, on West 72nd Street. That is one of the best residential sections of the city, and very close to the hospital where Israel will work. The manager showed me two lovely apartments. Each has two bedrooms, two baths, a spacious living/dining room, (a couch that opens for sleeping) and a bright and cheerful, fully equipped kitchen. The hotel provides daily maid service, linens, bedding and a large television. A luncheonette and restaurant are on the premises. You don't even have to make a cup of coffee, or cook an egg! By the way, do you know how to cook? If not, I'll be happy to teach you. You need not be concerned about food . . . NYC has 30,000 restaurants . . . I'm not joking . . . it's true.

Ruthchen, don't bring your two maids . . . not even one . . . they'll be a hindrance. The manager assured me that there would be several apartments for you to choose when you arrive. The hotel is only a few yards from the entrance to Central Park; an absolute gem. It has two zoos, (one for small children) lakes, swans, ducks, boating, ice-skating, restaurants, horseback riding, theater, walking and bicycle paths, concert shells and beautiful gardens . . . but no tennis courts or swimming pool. Shakespearean plays are performed on the Great Lawn in the summer, as well as all sorts of concerts . . . all free!

Ruthchen, you only need to bring your clothes. If you like to shop, this city is the greatest for that "sport." All you need is money!

We plan to pick you up at Newark Airport and bring you to our home for dinner. The following day I plan to be your chauffeur and tour guide. After that, you can make your own choices.

I can't wait.

Just a few more weeks before all of you will be here.

It will be marvelous.

Hugs and kisses to all, until we meet in person, real soon.

We'll be at the airport with a big station wagon.

Our dream IS coming true.

Keep dreaming.

Love to you all,
Helga

At last!

I remember her still as the young girl with the sweet round face, rosy cheeks and blond curly hair escaping out of her wool hat. But this time Ruth was an attractive, mature woman of thirty-four, when we spotted each other. As she stepped down from the plane, she waved both arms wildly, the strap of her purse dangling back and forth like a metronome. There was a beautiful smile on her expressive face.

In our haste to reach each other, we tripped, laughed and finally hugged and cried with joy. What had happened to those twenty-four years since we last saw each other? It felt so right . . . hugging like the young girls we used to be. This time I looked into her sparkling blue eyes and saw joy. How wonderful that we didn't need to suppress our emotions as we had to at the Berlin train station in 1938. On that auspicious day we were the ten-year-old best friends saying, *Auf Wiedersehen*. At the time we were thinking that perhaps we would never see each other again. Now we were grown women, wives and mothers, saying "hello" in English.

It is 1962.

We were in America.

Free . . . and together again.

Ruth and I were as excited as young lovers who hadn't seen each other for a long time. From the first moment we were so absorbed that we had forgotten to be polite and introduce our families to each other. They understood. Ruth introduced us to Israel, a gentle looking man of medium height and intelligent eyes that looked straight at me. Returning his gaze, I immediately felt . . . here was a person I hoped to get to know well. He was totally at ease. We didn't shake hands but immediately hugged, like family. I felt as if I had known him for years. *He's probably a good psychiatrist.*

Gaby, their thirteen-year-old daughter, had natural good looks, glowing rosy cheeks, and a lovely smile . . . just like her mother. Arturo, the eleven-year-old son, was a bit shy, still a small boy. He had his father's gentle, kind, intelligent look. The freckles on his nose made him look innocent.

My Jeffrey was ten years old, and Susie, seven. They both got into the contagious feeling of hugging and kissing their new friends. Al was in the background taking it all in, and then joined the celebration. Both Ruth and Israel spoke excellent English; their children did not, but would soon. Eventually we all got into the station wagon and were on our way from Newark to Queens. Suddenly I heard Ruth shouting, "Look . . . The Empire State Building!"

For the moment I was amazed that she recognized the landmark . . . but why not? Hadn't almost everyone seen a picture of the tallest building in the world? It thrilled me that they were so aware of the city and its landmarks. They were in awe of the skyscrapers, heavy traffic, impressive bridges, and the enormous number of people in the streets.

The four children, although not understanding each other's languages, were able to communicate in their impromptu sign language. Ruth and I had so much to say to each other that the men were not able to enter the conversation very much. After all, we had twenty-four years to catch up, and a whole year to devote to it.

I made dinner for the eight of us that evening. The table was already set when we entered the apartment. Ruth thought me a genius to be able to cook and serve without having a maid. She was impressed. I laughed. When Ruth ate the meat she was surprised by its tenderness.

"The seafood is excellent in Chile, but the meat needs to be tenderized . . . by pounding it forever."

"This is America, Ruth. You can get anything you wish . . . especially in New York."

<hr />

The first day together was absolutely perfect. The following morning we went to West 72nd Street to find an apartment. Initially, I drove around the East and West sides of Central Park and then took the road through the park itself. I wanted Ruth and the family to get a sense of the neighborhood. I then took them to the building that had the apartment I had described in my letter. The manager showed it to them, they all fell in love. The children were fascinated with the large television, and the couch that opened up.

What was on the agenda the following day? Ruth wanted to go shopping. She had heard that in the US there was something "new" . . . colorful plastic dishes! In Chile she had china and Limoge, (which I advised her not to bring) but no plastic. Gaby wanted a new white blouse. This was going to be easy. These requests were no challenge for me. I knew where to take them . . . RH. Macy & Co.

I knew that store inside and out. The enormity of the nine-story building, encompassing an entire square block impressed them. The escalator fascinated Gaby and Arturo. First we wanted to take care of the dishes. As soon as Ruth saw the first display she was in love. "Let's get this."

"Wait a minute," I said, "there are many different designs from other manufacturers you should look at."

I should have kept my mouth shut . . . but maybe not. The availability of so many choices was confusing. It made

Ruth's head spin. In Vina del Mar there are only "Mama and Papa" stores, with limited selections.

We decided to take a rest and go to the eighth floor where there is a popular, lovely, casual luncheonette. The waitress was helpful. She obviously had experience with foreign tourists. Gaby and Arturo enjoyed the atmosphere. I don't remember what we ordered, but I do recall the bottle of Heinz ketchup fascinated Arturo. Suddenly Israel hopped off the stool, excused himself, and went to greet a woman sitting opposite us. Ruth looked up and waved to her in recognition. Israel returned and related to me that the lady in question was the wife of the president of Chile, and she was in New York to select a trousseau for her daughter!

After this pleasant break, we went to another floor to look for a blouse for Gaby. That proved more difficult than choosing the plastic dishes. The teenager was overwhelmed. There were so many different styles; one more beautiful than the other. Gaby was mature and asked if she could come back another day . . . of course.

———

It was a joy to give dinner parties in honor of Ruth and her family. Our friends loved them, their stimulating conversations, sense of humor and varied topics of interest. Their social calendar filled up quickly . . . everyone wanted to host a party in their honor.

I made many recommendations, but the important one was to register the children into the New York public school immediately. I remember my Aunt Sophie doing the same for me three days after I arrived in the United States from Berlin in 1938. Ruth's children loved our schools and did very well. Gaby was thrilled that her intelligence was recognized, and she was put into an accelerated program. Arturo was fascinated by electronics. When the children left the States after one years' stay, they were fluent in English.

When summer was approaching I made another suggestion . . . send the children to sleep-away-camp. Years later, Gaby said camp was the highlight of her stay in America. Arturo loved American technology . . . television, toasters, subways, and ketchup. Ketchup brought back memories of how I fell in love at eleven, with the taste and artistic shape of the Heinz 57 bottle when I came to America. The mix of nationalities and races Arturo saw in New York intrigued him. Such a melting pot did not exist in Vina Del Mar.

To complete my list of suggestions, I proposed to Ruth and Israel to take a vacation at Grossingers, in the Catskill Mountains. No place in the world had the sports facilities, Broadway shows, enormous variety and quantity of food three times a day; all included in the price at the hotel.

Most of the guests who frequented this landmark hotel came with innumerable pieces of luggage. The majority of them changed their clothes a minimum of three times a day. That made the scene an on-going fashion show, around the pool, tennis courts, dining room, lounge, and of course the Broadway sized nightclub.

The clothes and food became an ongoing joke among television performers when Grossingers was mentioned in their repartee. Many comedians and singers got their initial break at the hotel. Talent agents were frequent guests, and recommended some of the personalities for the Jack Paar Show . . . the exposure helped careers take off.

The guests at the hotel were a mix of millionaires, politicians, lawyers, doctors, CEOs, theater and movie celebrities . . . and people from all walks of life, religions and finances. One didn't have to be rich to be a patron at Grossingers. Considering the amenities, it was an inexpensive place to vacation. Of course there were different rates depending on the rooms and the exposure. Single people were visitors with the hope of meeting the person of their dreams. Ruth remembers that vacation as an unbelievable experience. Israel enjoyed people watching.

For a fleeting moment before Ruth arrived in the states, I had a concern . . . would the eight of us get along? Although we were a diversified mix, like a puzzle with all the odd pieces, we fit together beautifully.

Ruth and I were amazed how much we recollected about our lives in Berlin. Sometimes we thought about former classmates and if one of us forgot a name, the other remembered. It was hard to realize that we had known each other for only five years until we were ten when we separated. For young children, life in Berlin was serious. We were aware of the stressful political environment. It was frightening. We felt that something was not right. Ruth's letters to me from Europe and Chile, when I was in New York, frequently mentioned the European situation.

American teenagers weren't aware what was going on across the Atlantic ocean, politically or geographically.

Often when our children were at school, the two of us had lunch at the Metropolitan Museum of Art, or MoMA (we looked at the art too)! It was fabulous.

The year passed quickly; too quickly. It was a fascinating experience for us all. Our friendship grew forever stronger. Finally the moment came to say goodbye. However; this time, it was not traumatic. We were sad to see Ruth's family leave, but we knew that we would see each other again. It would not take another twenty-four years.

Through the years Ruth and Israel came to visit frequently. In 1968, Al and I went to Gaby's wedding in Chile.

After thirty-four wonderful years together, Israel suddenly died. Ruth continued to visit me every two years. When she was in her middle seventies I knew that she was not well, but she didn't want to talk about it.

Ruth said she had a good life, and that Israel was the love of her being. In 2007, for her 80th birthday, I flew to Vina Del Mar to be her surprise present. She was so surprised . . . I was afraid she might have a heart attack. We didn't talk about our health, but about everything else. The ten days with Ruth were magical. After a glorious seventy-seven year friendship, Ruth died at eighty-two.

She is in my heart forever.

CAN YOU SPARE A . . . . ?

"Oh no!" I said to Al. "See that bum? Don't stop at the corner . . . drive slowly . . . make sure there's no policeman within sight . . . pass the red light. If you stop, he will suddenly approach with a filthy rag and 'clean' our windshield."

It was exasperating to drive through lower Manhattan, bordering on the Bowery, and have that happen again and again. And to boot, a tip was expected. A tip! For what . . . for dirtying our windshield?

It's 1958. I'm exhibiting my paintings at the Greenwich Village Outdoor Art Show. Artists prop their work against the New York University buildings, encompassing foursquare blocks, facing the famous Washington Square Park. It's a juried show, scheduled from Decoration Day, (aka Memorial Day) through June, and again from Labor Day, until the end of September. That time of year is the most glorious (weather-wise) to be in NYC.

Today, identifying someone as a Bowery bum is politically incorrect, but in the 1950s it was accepted vocabulary. The bums stayed in flop house hotels in the

Bowery, for ten cents a night. It was a ten-minute walk to Greenwich Village.

My husband and I drove our Plymouth station wagon, packed to the brim with my oil paintings, from Queens to my display area against one of the university buildings facing the park. I could not have asked for a better location, although the bums were around everywhere. I wasn't concerned; they were harmless.

On one occasion Al decided to clean his closet and get rid of suits that he had purchased after WWII. I was delighted. He put them into the back seat of the car, and we proceeded to the art show, knowing that some bum would appear to clean our windshield. And so it was. At a traffic light, just a few blocks from my exhibit space, one came . . . smiling . . . waving his dirty rag . . . as if it were the Stars and Stripes. Before he was able to touch our window, Al turned to the back seat and handed the bum six jackets and several pairs of pants. We were all delighted and as a bonus . . . our windows remained clean. Feeling proud about our donation, we proceeded to find a parking place.

Even fifty years ago, it was difficult to find spots in Greenwich Village. We drove around for blocks, making several turns, looking for a space. Suddenly I laughed. Al was so intent on his mission that he didn't see the comedy that was happening before my eyes. "Our" Bowery bum was already distributing the jackets and pants he had just gotten from us, to three bums. They were trying them on and being discreet . . . putting the "new" pants over the threadbare ones they were wearing. I was witness to a surreal fashion show. The men pranced . . . turned here and there . . . it was an improvised dance performance . . . with an imaginary mirror . . . pulling the fabric every which way to accommodate their body types. In turn, they critiqued each other's clothing as to fit and look. I heard "our" bum, a true entrepreneur, asking twenty-five cents per-garment!

During the Outdoor Art Show, the artists sat on the sidewalk in front of their work. I loved meeting the people who stopped to talk. Some were a bit strange, but the aspect of the unknown intrigued me. One man spoke to me for hours about art, politics, philosophy, and finally came to the subject on his mind. He proposed that he would buy three paintings if I agreed to spend the night with him! I showed him my wedding ring and told him I was flattered, but, "No, thanks." That incident made great conversation.

On another occasion, a bum asked me, "Lady would you give me fifty cents . . . I know it's a lot . . . but to tell you the truth . . . and I won't lie to you . . . it's really for wine . . . you'll help me celebrate this momentous event . . . my mother-in-law just died."

I looked him straight in the eyes. It was a great spiel but I wouldn't bite. My shopping bag was next to my chair.

"Hold on a minute," I said enthusiastically. Was there a twinkle in my eyes as I put my hand into the satchel and pulled out a bag of grapes?

"Here," I said emphatically as I handed him the fruit. "Make your own wine." I never saw him again.

In retrospect it made me sad when I thought about the bums. They were someone's children who became lost along the way. I engaged in conversations with some, and it was obvious that a good number were highly-educated.

For years there was one who walked the streets reciting Shakespeare; another sang famous arias.

One bum really fooled me. He had a great spiel . . . "I just found out that my grandmother died. I don't want money for wine. The funeral is in Brooklyn. I'll go by subway but I have no money. Could you give me two tokens?" (They were fifteen cents each.) I looked into my change-purse, benevolently handed him two, and I told him I was sorry about his grandmother.

An hour later, I went into a crowded bakery around the corner from my art space . . . and there was the bum . . . with a handful of subway tokens . . . trying to sell them for ten cents each!

THE RECLUSE

"Al, can you believe this . . . we have to climb another flight of stairs . . . that'll make it five! I'm exhausted . . . I thought I was in good shape."

"You're right. Let's rest a second."

"I didn't know that in 1959 some people still live like this . . . here in New York City. It feels like the 1900s . . . Left Bank . . . Paris."

"Do you hear the noise coming from the apartments?"

"Yes, it's pretty awful . . . I hope they have indoor plumbing. I've seen communal toilets in tenement buildings . . . it's an unhealthy way to live."

"They must have . . . I didn't see any toilets in the hallways."

"Thank goodness for that."

"Come on, Helga . . . be kind."

"Oh, Al . . . I have empathy. People who live this way probably don't have a choice."

We were invited to visit Al's first cousin, Heshy Shapinsky. He was one of four brothers of an eccentric family. Two brothers were well-known classical musicians. Murray played double bass with the Dallas Symphony, and Aaron was a cellist. Aaron started his career at an early age, played with Arturo Toscanini's Symphony Orchestra for NBC radio in the 1940s, and was under contract with the impresario, Sol Hurok. Heshy, an Abstract Expressionist painter, was a contemporary of de Kooning and Rothko. The youngest sibling, Bucky . . . was a truck driver. David, their father, was a designer in the garment industry. My son's middle name honors him. The mother of these four sons had a glorious voice. She was egocentric. If someone questioned me about who in this family was the most eccentric, it would be difficult to answer. They were all unique and lovable.

I was astounded by the invitation. As far as I knew, no family member had ever been invited to Heshy's apartment. Although I was a trained fashion designer, I painted since childhood. The first year I showcased my pallet-knife oil paintings at the Greenwich Village Outdoor Art Show was 1958, and I continued to do so for fifteen years. My exhibit space was in a great location . . . against one of the NYU buildings facing Washington Square Park. It was there that Heshy had seen my work. I was proud to display my talent. I was good . . . but not great.

After all that huffing and puffing up the steep stairs, we finally arrived on the fifth floor. I worried about the whipped cream cake I was carrying . . . bringing coffee cake would have been a better idea. Al knocked on Heshy's front door, and I wondered what was beyond the entrance.

The door opened, we stepped in, and found ourselves in the kitchen. Heshy and his wife, Kate, greeted us with open arms. She's tiny, a rail-thin woman with a beautiful face, bright blue eyes, long blond hair and the most outstanding glowing skin I have ever seen.

The kitchen was so small that the four of us touched, just standing . . . no place to move . . . no seating area. An open window made the street noise obtrusive. The wafting cooking odors escaped from the open windows of the many apartments, from the first to the fifth floor all merged, and were unpleasant by the time they reached the top floor. The biggest appliance in the kitchen was a sink, large and deep; it also was used for bathing and washing clothes. There was a water closet . . . toilet and sink.

Kate became flustered when I handed her the cake box. She graciously thanked me, turned to Heshy and whispered, "What shall we do? We only have two cups."

"I know, Sweetheart, I'll go next door and see if they can help us out . . . maybe they'll have a chair, too."

She led us through the archway into the living room. It had two windows, which gave the room some light; two mismatched old, unpainted wooden chairs, a bridge table and a milk crate. Period. There wasn't room for more. I watched Kate's graceful mobility, as she seemed to bend her body in half, to pick up something from the floor.

Heshy returned with two huge mugs; one metal, (probably army surplus) the other ceramic, and a wooden crate. I realized when we ate our dessert that a roasted chicken and a salad would have been a better choice for us to bring. Not until I saw their surroundings did I become aware of their meager existence.

I was anxious to see his art. But we had to wait . . . Heshy wasn't ready to expose his paintings. The conversation flowed pleasantly, from family, to literature, and the visual arts. He was impressed with my willingness to show my paintings at the Outdoor Art Show. I don't know what he thought of them or whether he admired my fortitude. Heshy divulged that no one had seen his work in years. His insecurity made me sad. *How will he ever sell if no one sees his work? Masterpieces can only be recognized if they're exposed to critics and art collectors.*

The scant amount of money Heshy earned came from teaching art to young children at a neighborhood Community Center. I knew that didn't pay well and I immediately thought of a way to help . . . *we'll bring our seven-year old son to his Saturday morning class.* Unfortunately that didn't work out. Jeffrey was more interested in teasing the girls than making art. Kate also taught, dance, to local children. She was not connected with any dance ensemble. St. Marks Place in the Lower East Side, where they lived, was a poor, neglected section of the city. How could they survive in a world where they both lacked self-recognition? Their rent was $12.50 a month, and even that small amount was a struggle. (I gained that information twenty-five years later.)

"Do you want to see my work, Helga?"

"Of course." Heshy took me into a tiny dark room that had only a bare 40-watt bulb. The paintings were stacked next to each other. It was difficult to see. He didn't take them into the living room where the light was better. I wanted to be optimistic, but all I saw were canvases in dark shades of blue . . . they all looked similar. For lack of visibility it was impossible to see his technique . . . brush strokes . . . pallet knife . . . collage? I was terribly disappointed. What could I tell him? He's such a recluse . . . he didn't even invite Al into the room to see his collection.

"Heshy, you must let people see your art. No one knows what you have . . . that you exist."

He said he would . . . but didn't. For years I didn't see him, or his art.

"Look! . . . My goodness . . . LOOK! This is hard to believe," I said to my friend. When I got to page forty-seven of the Dec.16, 1985 issue of *The New Yorker,* I couldn't contain myself. Lawrence Weschler, a reporter-at-large of this prestigious weekly magazine, wrote a *nineteen-page* article, (unusually long for this periodical) titled, *A Strange Destiny*. And indeed it was.

"This article was about OUR Heshy . . . renamed . . . HAROLD SHAPINSKY, in *The New Yorker* . . . unbelievable! What had Heshy done at sixty that he hadn't done in the last forty-five years? It's amazing . . . I'm thrilled for him! You must read it."

Heshy didn't do anything differently at sixty than the previous forty-five years, but destiny finally took a turn in his direction. A stranger, Akumal Ramachander, a native of Bangalore, India, called Lawrence Weschler at his *New Yorker* magazine office, told him that he had suddenly uncovered someone, something, extraordinary, and that he MUST see him immediately. Lawrence didn't take the call seriously, thanked him, and hung up. A few days later, a small, enthusiastic Indian man walked into Lawrence's office, unannounced. He graciously introduced himself; Lawrence Weschler being polite, asked Akumal what had he suddenly uncovered that was so important?

"Shapinsky!"

"WHO?*"* asked Weschler.

"Harold Shapinsky," he replied. "Abstract Expressionist painter, generation of de Kooning and Rothko, an undiscovered marvel, an absolute genius, completely unknown, utterly unappreciated. He lives here in New York City with his wife in a tiny one-bedroom apartment where he continues to paint as he has been doing for over forty-years, *like an angel.*" Akumal wrote Harold's address and phone number on a scrap of paper and shoved it into Lawrence's hand and said, "You *must* visit this Shapinsky fellow. He's a true find, a major discovery." He continued talking quickly before Weschler would ask him to leave his office. "It is my destiny to bring him to the attention of the world," said Akumal, the persistent salesman.

Weschler was speechless, but Ramachander was not. "You will see . . . this is an extraordinary discovery. As I say, I don't care about money. What's money? I do it because of my destiny."

A few weeks later, at seven in the morning, Akumal called Weschler at his apartment.

"Hello, Mr. Weschler, Akumal here, in Utrecht, Holland. You won't believe the good news! I took the slides of Shapinsky's work to the Stedelijk Museum in Amsterdam, and the curator there was amazed. He told me that I brought him the work of a great artist, that Shapinsky is a major find. I must tell you, I'm beginning to believe this is one of the great discoveries of the last decade." Weschler wasn't really eager to believe any of it. He hung up and went back to sleep.

A few days later Weschler's phone rang again, this time at his office. "Akumal again here, but this time in London. More good news! I visited the Tate . . . just walked in with no appointment, demanded to see the curator of modern art, refused to leave the waiting room until he finally came out . . . to humor me, I suppose, this silly little Indian fellow, you know . . . but presently he was *blown away*. Finally, he bows to me and says, 'Mr. Ramachander, you are right. Shapinsky is a terrific discovery.' Anyway, he gave me the name of a gallery . . . the Mayor Gallery. James Mayor, one of the top dealers in London . . . Warhol, Lichtenstein, Rauchenberg, first-rate. I went over there, and he, too, was flabbergasted. He's thinking about scheduling a show for the spring." Akumal talks so fast, . . . leaving words out . . . it's exhausting to listen to him.

Weschler found all of this fascinating, but didn't know what to make of it. He was too busy with deadlines to call or visit Shapinsky. The journalist wasn't sure if Shapinsky really existed.

Several days later the phone rang again at seven in the morning and Akumal in his excited voice informed Weschler, "British television! I showed the slides to some people at British Channel 4, and they loved them, right on the spot they committed themselves to doing a special, a one hour-long documentary to be ready in time for the show at the Mayor Gallery . . . on May 21st . . . Shapinsky's sixtieth birthday! They love the story, the idea of this unknown genius Abstract Expressionist and of the little Indian fellow and his destiny."

Actually the story begins here. Akumal had been traveling in India, Europe, and the United States. He was born into a poor family in India, but due to his belief in himself, and wanting to help people of the world in some measure, (not yet aware in which direction to go) persevered and became an academic. Akumal became a professor of elementary English at the College of Agricultural Sciences in Bangalore. When prodded to acknowledge his position there, he said it was insignificant.

He found himself in India, meeting a professor of sociology from Kansas State University. Through this odd encountering, he was invited to the University of Chicago to lecture on Indian politics and cinema; an odd combination. It's a far-fetched story. Truly serendipity.

It was at a University of Chicago gathering that Akumal met twenty-four-year-old David Shapinsky . . .

Heshy's son . . . who was doing graduate work in American diplomatic history. Since the Indian man traveled extensively, he was interested in the young man's knowledge. The following day they ran into each other on campus. David asked Akumal if he would join him to have coffee. He agreed. At their *tete a tete*, David talked about his father's paintings and asked this energetic little man to look at Heshy's art slides.

Akumal was *blown away* . . . an expression he used frequently pertaining to Heshy's art. He was extremely impressed, told David that he felt within a year his father's paintings would be shown at a world-class gallery; maybe not in America, but in Europe. He wasn't sure about the New York market, having more familiarity with the European art scene.

Weschler received a phone call from Akumal a few weeks later.

By now he knew the man's habit, and was not surprised to hear from him. But this time Akumal was in New York . . . actually he was in Heshy's apartment. He was very emphatic . . . "Weschler you must come to Shapinsky's apartment immediately, and see it all for yourself." And so the journalist went.

From the 1985 *New Yorker* article I quote Weschler's first meeting with my cousin Harold (Heshy) Shapinsky.

"I pushed a doorbell and was buzzed in: *(didn't have that modern convenience when Al and I visited in 1958)* a five-story walkup; steep steps." *(No change there)* Weschler described the tiny apartment, overflowing with the film crew's equipment for a documentary. "The only narrow bed was covered with coats and movie paraphernalia; the tiny bedroom used as a studio.

"A very dignified and dapper-looking, English gentleman had spread several paintings about the bedroom floor and was crouched down making careful selections as the television crew peered over his shoulder. I spotted Akumal, who was beaming. Next to him stood a soft, slightly stooped, fairly rumpled, gray-bearded old man, wrapped in a moth-eaten wool sweater and puffing cherry-sweet tobacco smoke into the air from the bowl of a well-chewed pipe.

"'Ah, Mr. Weschler, I want you to meet Harold Shapinsky.'" *Of course, who else could that person have been, but our cousin Heshy? He must have aged a lot in the twenty-five years since I saw him, to be described as an 'old man.' He's only sixty.)*

"The cameraman asked if he could have Shapinsky and his wife stand by the window for a moment. James Mayor spoke into the mike, 'Most amazing story. I mean, an artist of this caliber . . . living like this . . . dirt poor . . . completely unknown . . . *living in a virtual garret* five stories above a Japanese restaurant I've been to dozens of times. Quite good Japanese restaurant, by the way." James Mayor continued, "I must say, when Akumal brought me those slides I was astonished. I mean this art business can get one pretty jaded after a while. One gets to feeling one has seen it all. You begin to despair of ever again encountering anything original, powerful, real. I haven't felt a buzz like this in a long time.'"

Reading Weschler's article, I realized Heshy's financial situation had not changed in the last twenty-five years. Weschler mentioned that he went to Harold's house several times and there were never enough cups or chairs . . . an ancient stereo was used for seating. Reading that description, I chuckled, (*Yes, that's how it was two and a half decades ago)* but on further thought I became sad. The manner in which Harold pursued his art made his life difficult . . . he truly lived it . . . the starving artist. He wrote that Kate and Harold slept on a thin mattress that they stacked in a closet by day. Lack of money also affected his health. He was thin and gaunt. His wife thought he looked like a figure in an El Greco painting. Heshy was malnourished. I don't know if that was due to lack of money or lack of interest in food, probably both.

The family once heard a story, years after the fact: Heshy was a young twenty-year old artist, recently moved to St. Marks Place . . . had no money and barely survived eating a bag of peanuts a day. His older married brother, Aaron, came to visit, saw Heshy's horrible physical condition, too weak to get out of bed; and took him home for the summer to be with his family in Long Island. With loving care he improved. After several months he returned to his tenement apartment, only to find that his landlord had trashed everything, including *throwing his life's work of paintings out!* His brother had forgotten to pay the $12.50 monthly rent!

I learned more about his youth from Weschler's article then our family had ever known. Heshy's parents divorced when he was a young teenager. He admitted to Weschler that his was an unhappy childhood. His mother loved music but had no appreciation for the visual arts. She was known to throw his paintings out. But more bizarre was his stepfather, who on occasion took Heshey's artwork and then painting over them! After spending time at New York museums and galleries, he became intrigued by Picasso and Cézanne's work. Heshy vowed at fifteen to become an artist, leave home, and live alone.

The time came for Harold's exhibit . . . twenty-two paintings at the Mayor Gallery in London. The price was set at $20,000-$30,000 per painting by John Mayor and his partner, the gallery owners. If Harold had painted on larger canvases the prices would have been higher. When interviewed Shapinsky explained that he lived in a small apartment, had little money for art supplies and for that reason often painted on brown paper.

Shapinsky's relationship with Akumal was unique. They never talked about money. Akumal wanted none, although he was not well off financially. Shapinsky was his destiny. Kate and Harold insisted, that Akumal receive a percentage of everything sold from the Mayor Gallery show and all others to come. He was embarrassed by the offer but Harold and Kate insisted.

Harold had no knowledge of the selling price of his work. That information didn't interest him . . . he didn't care about money. This trip to London was a first for him, Kate and their son, David. They had never been out of the country. The day of the opening Akumal realized that Harold didn't own a suit. They went shopping. For the gala opening event Harold wore a gray flannel suit with blue canvas deck shoes!

He was interviewed by many journalists, but none as famous as the writer Salman Rushdie, a friend of Akumal. Rushdie admired Harold the first time they met, described him as: "Reserved, measured and withdrawn. He was always gentle and polite, but he was subdued; indeed, at times his restraint verged on the spooky. He answered questions in a flat, becalmed voice with simple sentences often consisting of just one or two words ("Yes, marvelous," or "Truly gratifying.")

Robert Motherwell recalls Harold with big horn glasses, very pale and thin. When questioned about the artist, Motherwell said, "There was no question with Shapinsky . . . the talent and dedication were real. The main thing I remember about him is how terribly intense he was . . . a combination of extreme intensity and shyness."

Life hadn't changed for Harold in forty years except the Waldorf Cafeteria, at Sixth Avenue and Eight Street, no longer existed. That had been the artists hang out in the 1950's. Harold described it well: "There was a tremendous camaraderie among the artist. We were putting our all into paintings, into the activity of painting itself. We'd get together at the old Waldorf Cafeteria, and talk about the mission of painting. Nobody gave a thought to money, or to exhibiting, or even to selling the work. It was a pure scene." Rothko, de Kooning, Pollack, Kline, Motherwell,

Shapinsky, all met there. It was their indoor left Bank, Paris Café, in Greenwich Village. "We weren't in the 1950's Abstract Expressionists . . . that designation would only come later. We were just *painters*."

———

A COMPLETE SELL-OUT OF SHAPINSKY'S PAINTINGS AT THE MAYOR GALLERY!

———

Akumal informed Harold that the next big show with fifteen pieces of his work, with increased prices, is scheduled at a prime gallery in Cologne, Germany.

———

After the huge success, Harold had only one question for Akumal, his advisor, "Can I afford a Burberry raincoat?"

Harold and Kate moved to a condominium that had an elevator.

———

Harold (Heshy) Shapinsky died in 2004, at age 79. *The New York Times* had an impressive obituary about him.

The Bachelor

My cousin Moe had been engaged four or five times, but never married. Moe and my mother were first cousins, born just before the turn of the 20th century in Eastern Europe. Their parents and siblings moved to Berlin, Germany, when they were in their teens. Because of their similar ages, they had a very close relationship, like loving siblings. My mother introduced Moe to many of her girlfriends, all of whom had the same backgrounds, smart, pretty, and were delighted to meet him. He was intelligent, a good conversationalist and well-liked by young and old. Dominated by his Alfred E. Neuman ears, his looks were not outstanding but his sparkling blue eyes, easy smile and friendly personality were.

One by one, he became engaged to my mother's friends. Each time Moe proposed marriage, his friends and relatives were elated, always hoping that this time would be "it." However, in each case, after a period of time, the women approached Moe to set a wedding date, but he was always evasive.

The young ladies all knew each other. I'm of the opinion that they "waited in the wings" for Moe's refusal, so that they got a chance to be "next." Did Moe think that he was at a dance, just filling the young ladies dancing cards? Was he playing a game, boosting his ego . . . the available bachelor? No commitment came from him. My mother eventually became embarrassed about her cousin's behavior. She probably also ran out of suitable girlfriends.

After some time the young women realized that there was no hope in pursuing Moe. The amazing part of the saga was that they tearfully said goodbye, but remained friends. Within a few years all of my mother's girlfriends met other men and married. Moe remained the eligible bachelor. Even I fell for his charm. When I was eight years old, I told Moe, "I love you. Wait for me. When I'm old enough I want to marry you."

"Thank you, Sweetheart. Don't worry," he said. "All the ladies who wanted to marry me couldn't wait and eventually married someone else. So will you."

And so it was.

In 1934, when Hitler was flexing his muscles, Moe left Berlin, and moved to the U.S. My mother's brother Morris, in Bridgeport, Connecticut, sponsored him. Initially Moe lived with Uncle Morris (his first cousin), his wife, Sophie, and their two children. Uncle Morris brought Moe into his lingerie manufacturing business. He learned quickly and worked hard. Morris taught him well. Promotions came quickly for this bright young man. Uncle Morris elevated him to plant manager, and eventually to partner. In 1938, the business had 300 workers.

When Moe felt financially secure, he rented a room in a private home from an elderly couple. He was frugal and never felt the need to own anything . . . except watches. He had twenty men's watches, but always wore the same one. His one big expense was the purchase of a new car that simplified getting to Aunt Sophie's home for dinner every night of the week. Uncle Morris enjoyed having conversations with Moe and Aunt Sophie had someone else who appreciated her delicious home-cooked meals. Everyone was happy.

Moe visited my family in Manhattan several times a year. We welcomed those weekends because he was always amenable to joining us at restaurants, concerts, or the theatre. Frequently my mother made dinner parties. Moe knew all of my parent's friends, and they always included him in their get-togethers. Life was livelier when Moe was around.

When he was in his early fifties, my mother again tried to be a matchmaker. Twenty years had passed since he came to America, and as far as we knew, he never dated. Mother introduced him to a distant cousin who lived in New Jersey. Rose was in her late thirties, well educated, with a responsible job that paid handsomely. She was tall and thin, lacked personality and sadly, was unattractive. I felt sorry for her, and probably my mother did too. As an unmarried woman she lived in a big private house with her parents, and looked like the stereotypical spinster one sees in the movies.

On one occasion I accompanied my parents on a visit to New Jersey. The interior of their house was as depressing as Rose was unexciting. The wooden furniture was dark and massive. That feeling continued with the gloomy over-stuffed upholstered chairs and couch. The heavy dark green and brown tweed drapes that were kept partially drawn made the room gloomy. The house smelled old. I couldn't wait to get home. Rose's parents were of advanced age and desperately wanted to see their only daughter married. Sad. They mentioned a large dowry to my mother. That must have motivated Moe. He started dating her.

For months, every Saturday morning, Moe drove from Bridgeport to New Jersey to visit Rose. One weekend when my family visited Morris and Sophie, Moe stayed on to see us. We sat in Uncle Morris's cozy den, on a well-worn comfortable brown leather couch, facing the love seat. Morris, a large man, with a jolly face, sat on the big wing chair. There was no mistaking, he was the boss. Aunt Sophie, known for her hospitality, always had goodies on the large cocktail table. Crystal dishes were filled to the brim with nuts, dried apricots, chocolates, and a large silver bowl contained shiny polished apples, pears and oranges. I remember as a young child polishing the apples by rubbing them against my dress on my backside. It brings back loving memories. I loved hearing the noise of the metal nutcracker when the walnuts got crushed and the shells flew all over the table. Her display of food always looked like a staged still life to be painted on canvas. During the conversations Aunt Sophie unobtrusively peeled oranges in unbroken spirals, and offered the segments to us. The room had the pleasant smell of citrus.

The interrogation began when my mother asked Moe, "Where do you go with Rose when you visit her?"

"Nowhere. We stay in her living room and listen to the radio."

"You mean you don't take her to a movie, a concert, or a restaurant?"

An emphatic "No" was his reply.

My mother was incredulous at his statement.

Moe claimed that Rose's parents were so delighted with his company, that the four of them sat in the parlor, listened to music, and talked for hours. We were amazed. Then the inquisition started in earnest. Everyone in the room, including me, wanted to know if Moe intended to marry her.

"No," he said. "She wouldn't be a suitable wife." After that callous statement, the questions came flying from everyone.

"Why do you see her then?" Morris asked.

Sophie exclaimed, "You're raising her hopes. Why do you visit her . . . for a free meal? You get that at my house every day without traveling!"

Everyone in the room was furious with Moe. I was married, in my late twenties, and the conversation astounded me. This was a sad scenario. I felt incredibly bad for Rose. *Life is unfair . . . she deserves better.* Listening to the heated conversation was both fascinating and disturbing. I never realized how insensitive Moe was. Everyone agreed that he must stop leading Rose on. He must stop seeing her. Moe became angry with all of us.

"She'll be upset," was his comment.

I couldn't believe what I had just heard, from a person I had respected until that moment. No longer was I able to contain myself. I raised my voice and stated, "Moe, you bet she'll be upset! Who wouldn't be? She's been waiting for the prince, you, to save her . . . to sweep her off her feet . . . whisk her off to Bridgeport . . . and then down the aisle."

How long did he think he could string her along? Didn't he have any feelings? I kept thinking . . . traveling every weekend . . . to get a free meal . . . was this a power trip? And what about her parents? Were they too intimidated to say anything to Moe . . . fearing he would run away . . . never to be seen again? Was this chapter about my family written by Isaac Bashevis Singer or Tennessee Williams?

It took some time for the jury of Moe's closest relatives to convince him: Be honorable. Stop the charade. Reluctantly he listened.

Poor Rose. She never married.

Moe had a plan. He had many nieces and nephews in Europe. He hoped that when WWII was over, he would sponsor all of them and bring them to the States. They would be the children he never had. He wanted desperately to give them the opportunity to get a good education. However, his dream was not to be. When he learned they were all victims of the Holocaust, Moe went into deep mourning. Until the day he died, he always wore a solid black knitted tie.

He was frugal . . . hardly spent any money. My uncle's business was successful. Moe was doing well financially. His rent was cheap and he ate dinner at Sophie's house every night.

It amazed me when I talked to Aunt Sophie on the telephone about her and Morris going on vacation with my parents. Sophie said, she couldn't.

"Why not?"

"Where will Moe eat dinner when Morris and I are away?" was her explanation. I nervously laughed, and accused her of being ridiculous.

Instead of going on vacations each summer when the factory was closed for two weeks, Moe checked himself into a New York hospital for a complete physical check-up. We couldn't believe he would do such a thing. He was pampered by the nurses and fed three meals a day. The tests showed that he was healthy. Moe was happy. The two weeks at the hospital were a bargain compared to a stay at Grossinger's, in the Catskills.

For decades I enjoyed my family weekends with Sophie and Morris. Moe was always present, and I could rely on his contribution to the diverse conversations. The subject matter ranged from politics, family gossip, food, entertainment, fashions, religion or finance. There were arguments too. Morris usually won . . . my mother and Moe came in second. The debates were stimulating; never threatening, and I enjoyed the banter thoroughly. Aunt Sophie on occasion made a comment, but being the hostess was her claim to fame.

Sophie announced on one of my visits that her nineteen-year-old niece, who lived in Sao Paulo, Brazil, was coming to stay with her and Morris, for the summer. Regina was a talented pianist and hoped to be accepted at the Julliard School of Music. I liked her immediately. Just looking into her eyes conveyed her intelligence. Her English was excellent, and I was impressed by her maturity. To round out the equation, she was a natural beauty, a-la Ava Gardner. Having come from Sao Paulo, a cosmopolitan city of six million people, she found Bridgeport provincial, was anxious for the summer to be over, and to live in Manhattan. Regina knew what she wanted, which I found commendable for someone so young.

She never got to New York. To everyone's surprise, Moe announced that he and Regina had fallen in love. At sixty-nine, he was half a century older than she. Sophie and Morris were overwhelmed. Things went badly when Regina's parents were informed that their talented, beautiful daughter wanted to marry a man fifty years her senior. They were furious. The parents' anger was directed at Sophie.

"Sophie, you are my sister . . . how could you have permitted them to fall in love . . . and, in your own house? We trusted you with our child," Regina's father screamed into the telephone from Brazil.

The situation presented enormous friction in the family. Regina's father traveled to Bridgeport to convince his daughter to return with him to Sao Paulo. She refused to leave Moe.

For three decades Moe had occupied the same chair at Sophie's dining table every night. He stopped coming. The atmosphere became exceedingly uncomfortable. Regina moved out. Sophie felt betrayed. Morris was furious with everyone. The warm, friendly house in Bridgeport suddenly felt like a morgue.

What did a young sophisticated teenager see in a sixty-nine year old man? Moe was old enough to be her grandfather. I liked Moe but couldn't see the attraction. He was just an ordinary, nice man; not handsome, nor sophisticated, talented, famous, exceedingly wealthy, or out of this world charismatic. For decades I thought of him as asexual. For him, this romance could have been his last hurrah. Remember the many times he got engaged in his youth? But for Regina . . . was it his money . . . did she wish to get away from her family in South America? These questions were never answered. Regina had her young life ahead of her . . . she chose Moe.

They eloped.

It was the most sensational tidbit to appear in the Bridgeport newspaper: *Bachelor Marries Teenager Half Century His Junior.* I would have been willing to be a witness at their marriage, but they never contacted me; or anyone else.

Moe bought a luxurious condo in a new apartment building. An interior designer furnished it completely, down to the towels, dishes and ashtrays. As a wedding gift, Moe gave Regina the keys to a brand new Cadillac. Finally he was spending his money; and enjoyed doing so. Within three years, Moe became the proud father of two beautiful girls, eighteen months apart. He glowed . . . he was alive. In his seventies, he had a beautiful family of his own. I was thrilled to see him happy.

It didn't last.

Four years after their marriage, Regina asked for a divorce. The family was totally astounded. Our hearts went out to Moe. His relationship with Morris and Sophie remained strained but they were sad for him. No one asked him, "What happened?"

Moe was devastated. He moved out. In order to see his babies every day, he bought a studio apartment, in the same building. At least he had experienced love.

Five years after the marriage, Moe, age seventy-four, died of a heart attack.

SUSIE
AND
JEFFREY

Sunshine and Midnight

Is this for real . . . my New York City hippie kids . . . on a farm in Sarasota, Florida? It's 1974 and I'm visiting Jeffrey, and his sister Susie, for the first time in their new dwelling. Actually, the dwelling isn't new . . . it's probably one of the oldest houses in Sarasota . . . but for them it's a new residence. The brother and sister are living together once again . . . since leaving their big city nest.

Both of my children left the Big Apple to go to college out west . . . Jeffrey to Lake Forest College in Illinois; Susie, three years later, to the University of Colorado, in Boulder. After two years, Jeffrey left college, bought an old truck that he lovingly named Mister Green. He traveled here and there, looking for something of interest to grab him. On his way east he noticed that Mr. Green was thirsty. He found himself in Jerome, Arizona, looking for a gas station. There was none. In 1952 Jerome had been abandoned by Phelps-Dodge when the copper mine ran dry. In its prime the population boasted 15,000 . . . now it was down to fifty-eight residents.

A great percentage of the people were hippies doing craftwork. That appealed to Jeffrey. He stayed for two years; learned to tool leather . . . made exquisite briefcases, (for imagined lawyers and executives) wallets, belts, and whatever else intrigued him. Rent was cheap. Obviously Jerome had no industry. There were an enormous number of abandoned mansions that in their hey-day, 1880s-1952, Phelps-Dodge executives had occupied. The real estate was still owned by the mining company but was not for sale.

Jeffrey rented a store, and lived in a sleeping loft that he designed. In town he met another hippie, Peggy, a jewelry designer. They became a couple, and in less than two years they packed everything into Mr. Green (even hippies realize their need to eat) and left Jerome. Peggy, a Sarasota native, was certain that Jeffrey would find employment in her birthplace. Enter Jeffrey, the first of the Harris clan to settle in Sarasota . . . it was 1973.

Really . . . is this for real? Am I seeing right? I came to visit my children in their home. I heard scratching sounds in Susie's bedroom, coming from her closet. I opened the door . . . and what did I see . . . not shoes and clothes . . . but hay and shredded newspapers on the floor, along with the sweetest kid (baby goat) looking at me with soulful eyes! I was flabbergasted. This is not what a New York apartment dweller expects to see in a closet. Susie explained that milking goats couldn't nurse their young; therefore, she was the provider and fed the baby with a nipple attached to a Coke bottle. I found it all charming but wondered where the bottle came from? Coke had been taboo in our house, and I knew she didn't drink it.

Their new residence was referred to as the Farmhouse. It sat on fifty-six acres of citrus grove on a dirt road north of Lockwood Ridge, now a sprawling subdivision called Oak Run. My children were in heaven living at the Farmhouse. In no time they had two horses, chickens, rooster, guinea hens, bees, ducks, many goats, a dog and a cat. My city daughter, now wearing overalls and her hair in braids, milked her brood twice a day. Her clients were people allergic to cow's milk. Susie's enterprise did not cover her measly fifty dollar monthly rent contribution. To subsidize her expenses she worked as a waitress in a cheap breakfast joint. She hated it. But when Susie was offered a job at a good restaurant where her tips would make my hippie "rich," she refused because she was asked to shave her legs and wear their fitted outfit.

She loved her goats. Sunshine and Midnight were her favorites. There were always people about and life was fun. Susie even made the headlines in *The Sarasota Herald Tribune,* when one of her goats gave birth to triplets.

I loved staying at their house. Truthfully, I envied my children's freedom. To describe the Farmhouse is difficult. It had three tiny bedrooms, and a small living room with a fireplace . . . a fireplace in Florida? I laughed the first time I saw it but welcomed it on some winter visits. There was a kitchen, the largest room in the house, with old funky appliances that worked, and which were used daily. The smell of freshly baked bread gave the atmosphere a homey, loving, feeling. Jeffrey converted the porch into a workshop for his carpentry.

A staircase at a side of the living room led to a room above, the size of the entire house. That's where I slept. The view was unlike what I was used to in the big city. It felt like heaven. A door to nowhere faced me ... unless one wanted to jump two stories to the ground. It was Jeffrey's idea to someday build a porch. Probably that's how the whole house grew, without planning; just stick another room onto the existing one, when needed. Of course there was no air-conditioning or heat, except for the fireplace.

Jeffrey started building exotic wood furniture, and Susie was happy with her goats. On one of my visits I saw a kid on the kitchen stove ... and to think that I taught my children to keep their elbows off the table! Things certainly had changed ... and I loved it.

The house was always filled with interesting people. On another visit I was fortunate to be part of the group to witness the marriage of two of their friends around the great oak tree. As a fashion designer I was interested to see the mode of dress for the festivities. I was not disappointed ... denims, cut offs, spray-painted tops, long skirts, overalls, long hair, braids, (for both sexes) beards and smiling faces all around. *WWD (Woman's Wear Daily)* didn't have a journalist to report this happening. They should have. What they would have witnessed ... the bride and groom dressed in velvet, as Romeo and Juliet, each holding a flowerpot in their arm. At the end of the ceremony the newlyweds kissed and then planted the containers at the base of the oak tree.

"That was charming," I told Jeffrey.

He looked at me in amazement and said, "Mom, don't you know what that is?" I gazed at him . . . he had that impish look . . . then I put two and two together! *Wow . . . I hope they don't get arrested!*

Underneath the love Susie and Jeffrey had for the Farmhouse there always was the underlying fear of what the future would hold. When they rented the property, the owner told them that eventually the acreage would be sold. My children wanted to live there forever . . . nothing is forever.

After three years of magic the dreaded news came . . . they had to leave their beloved Farmhouse. Although they knew that this moment would come, they were devastated. Where could they find a place to duplicate this environment?

Susie was especially bereft. She had to give up her goats, including Sunshine and Midnight. Sweet notices were put on community boards and in health food stores about selling her "babies." I think up to that period of her life, this situation was the hardest for her to face . . . no more Sunshine and Midnight. They were her loves.

I was present when three large men dressed in long white robes came to the Farmhouse to buy the goats. They looked ominous. Susie had strong feelings that they belonged to a religious cult who wanted the animals for sacrificial purposes. She made eye contact with me, and then looked them straight in the face and said, "The goats are not for sale." The men didn't believe her and increased their original offer. I felt uneasy. They then quoted a higher price, but couldn't coerce my Susie. Reluctantly they left. I was frightened thinking the worst. Luckily we never saw them again. Susie gave the goats to people who had lots of land and who promised to keep them as pets.

In 1977, Jeffrey and Susie found houses next door to each other on Oak Street. I find it interesting that my children always lived together or next to each other except when they were in college. Thanks Peggy, for leading the way for the Harris family to live in Sarasota.

After Sixty Years . . . Back To Berlin

"**Y**ou can go to Berlin . . . Free!"

Who is this woman, with a distinct German accent? I've have never seen her before and why did she approach me? Her announcement stunned me . . . her presence unnerved me. What a yenta. The accent immediately put me on the defensive. I don't trust older people with a German accent . . . it makes me wonder . . . what were you . . . and your family doing . . . during the Holocaust? I felt myself getting angry, and knew that wasn't fair. I admit . . . I have a hang-up.

My first thought: *I'm not ever going to step on German soil again. I have no interest in visiting Berlin, my birthplace. Furthermore, I have no allegiance to the Fatherland . . . nothing to be proud of . . . only hatred. They didn't want me . . . actually they wanted to be rid of me. Why would I wish to return?*

In 1986, while standing on line at a Miami department store to pay for a purchase, I heard "Helga," called by a friend. A stranger ahead of me on line, turned, and asked me whether I had been born in Germany since my name is common there. I had no intention of answering. Usually I denied such inquiries . . . being glib is easier than explaining the when, and where. Furthermore, I was sensitive to the possibility of being identified as German, and shuddered at the thought. I'm NOT German! For reasons I cannot comprehend, this time I answered truthfully.

With that knowledge, the woman told me, "If you're Jewish, born in Berlin, emigrated from Germany between 1935-1945, are over sixty, and have never returned to your birthplace, then you're eligible to visit there with your spouse . . . for a week . . . ALL expenses paid . . . including generous daily spending money." She was out of breath after that complete explanation.

Can what she said be a fact? "Why?" I questioned.

"The Berlin office of Der Regierende Burgermeister von Berlin, Senatskanslei-Protokoll (Berlin Mayor's Office) invites people with your background as a gesture of goodwill."

What a clever German public relations ploy.

She continued, "The young Berliners wish to make amends, to ask for forgiveness for the atrocities their forefathers had been involved in." Was I ready to accept the proposal . . . to forgive . . . let my guard down?

"I don't want to return to Berlin. I would feel like a traitor."

"Don't be foolish," the woman retorted. "It's a wonderful trip. My husband and I just came back two weeks ago. It was wonderful. A non-Jewish group sponsors the organization. Think about it. It costs you nothing. I'll give you my card. Call me . . . I have the contact number. No hurry. This process takes several years from the time you apply, until the date of your visit. Take my advice . . . get on the list. All you need is proof that you were born in Berlin. You can make your final decision when Protokoll communicates with you . . . years from now."

Amazing. You never know how, or, when, your life can take an interesting turn. I took her card and thanked her. Then my thoughts wandered: Wouldn't it be wonderful if Ruthchen and I could meet in Berlin as elders, and walk the same streets we had skipped along when we were ten-year-old best girlfriends in 1938? It was not to be. Ruth and her husband had been to Berlin several years earlier and therefore were ineligible.

A few months later, on my 60th birthday, I remembered the conversation with the woman in the department store. I called her. She remembered me and was enthusiastic about my change of heart. It was my daughter, Susie, who talked me into pursuing the trip. Her "hook" that got me to rethink the situation was, "Mom, they owe it to you!"

Certainly the price was right but I feared that the expression, "There's no free lunch" could haunt me.

For years I had corresponded with Mr. Nemitz, my contact in the Berlin Mayor's Office. Annually I asked him what my standing on the list was. The answer was always the same; "Be patient." Since I had no spouse I requested that Susie accompany me. Their response was that she could, IF she paid her own way . . . but they would gladly furnish her with all the same cultural event tickets that I would receive. I was furious. I felt that under the circumstances they "owed" me two reservations. No . . . Protokoll would pay only if I had a husband. I reasoned; why should I be penalized because I didn't have a spouse . . . my daughter would share my hotel room with me? Their answer remained negative . . . they had rules and regulations. Susie implored me to stop pushing. She was fearful that I might jeopardize my position and be crossed off the list. At this point I was so angry that I didn't care, and thought: *Who needs them . . . it's blood money.*

Ten years later, in 1997, I received an invitation informing me that since I will be seventy years that year, I could bring my daughter to Berlin, with all expenses paid.

I won! But why didn't I feel like a winner? The question was . . . do I really want to go? Even under those conditions I was not enthusiastic. Susie persuaded me to stop being stubborn and accept the invitation. Having her along might take the edge off, and it would be a great experience for her. My daughter knew me as a positive person, except when it came to my German suffering. Perhaps on this trip she would begin to understand my behavior toward everything German.

A definite advantage to this journey was Ati, a non-Jewish German young woman (my children's age) I had met in Miami in 1977, and with whom I had become very friendly. She now lived in Berlin. I trusted her; so much so, that I told her of my feelings against Germans . . . and this wonderful young German woman . . . understood me. Susie had met Ati several times on her visits to Miami, and liked her. Ati was thrilled when she heard that we were coming to Berlin, and immediately told us that she would take time off from work. Her idea was for us to inform her of our daily itinerary, and let her know which points of interest we'd like to return to. Of course, Ati, the greatest tour guide (not her profession) would make certain that nothing was missed. This is a person with enormous interest in life and energy to match.

The following are my journal entries:

September 7-17, 1997.

For weeks my friends had asked me if I was excited about the impending trip. "No." I was skeptical. Two weeks ago I received a packet from Mr. Nemitz, which contained plane tickets, hotel reservations and the daily itinerary. Also included was a list of ninety names, ages, and current addresses, and those from the time we lived in Berlin, in the 1930s. The purpose was to possibly find someone we knew . . . remembered. It was an international assemblage of people from six continents and fifteen countries, including New Zealand. Everyone in the group was bringing a family member.

As of now my body has not reacted in any way. I have never been so lethargic. It's twenty-four hours before Susie and I leave and the adrenaline still hasn't kicked in. A friend called inquiring, "How are you doing?"

"I still haven't packed . . . and I even went to the movies this afternoon." She was shocked, and so was I. I was holding back . . . but what was I afraid of?

It was departure day and Jeffrey came to wish us farewell. "Mom, are you excited?"

"No."

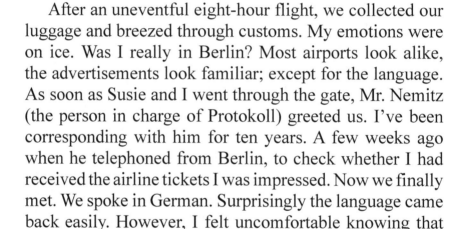

After an uneventful eight-hour flight, we collected our luggage and breezed through customs. My emotions were on ice. Was I really in Berlin? Most airports look alike, the advertisements look familiar; except for the language. As soon as Susie and I went through the gate, Mr. Nemitz (the person in charge of Protokoll) greeted us. I've been corresponding with him for ten years. A few weeks ago when he telephoned from Berlin, to check whether I had received the airline tickets I was impressed. Now we finally met. We spoke in German. Surprisingly the language came back easily. However, I felt uncomfortable knowing that Susie was left out of the conversation. When I mentioned that fact to Mr. Nemitz, he immediately switched to English. He personally brought us to our hotel.

Our room was large, light and cheerful. It was obvious that everything had been arranged. On our beds we found maps of the city, a variety of books pertaining to Berlin and Jewish activities of interest, listings of kosher restaurants, grocery stores and synagogues. Grocery stores . . . that took me by surprise since all our meals were taken care of. A generous check for daily spending money, and planned programs for the week were also included. Nothing was omitted.

I relaxed on the bed and daydreamed. The last image I had of Berlin was being on the railroad station platform in April 1938, bidding a tearful *Auf Wiedersehen*, to my best friend Ruthchen. We were ten-years-old, and had known each other since kindergarten. I intend to visit that train station. But sadly, there would be no Ruth with me. She lives in Chile since 1939, and is waiting for news from me.

Sixty-years later, I'm in Berlin with Susie and kept asking myself: Am I really in Berlin? It felt strange. I felt strange. I tried to recollect the faces of my twenty-two classmates but could visualize only ten. As far as I know, five of us have survived the Holocaust. What do I expect to find? . . . someone from my past to suddenly appear on the streets of Berlin, and call out, "Helga, Helga, look . . . I'm here!" After more than a half a century, how much do I . . . would I . . . wish to remember?

The day we arrived was a free day. Susie and I looked at the map and found the bank where we could convert our traveler's checks into marks, and also cash the check from Protokoll for our daily expenses. Berlin is a walking city, very much like Manhattan, which pleased us. We were informed that it is safe for two women to stroll in the neighborhood of the hotel in the evenings.

Susie got excited when I recognized some of the street names. She reasoned that I must have walked there as a child and made me feel like a celebrity. I noticed KaDeWe, the largest department store, like Macy's, Herald Square. That's where my mother and her friends often took me and Ruthchen, for Kaffe, Kuchen, and Schlagsahne,(coffee, cake and whipped cream) on many weekends. Of course I took Susie to retrace my steps. It was a disappointment. The store was in the midst of their End of Summer Sale . . . everything was tossed about . . . not unappealing. In my memory KaDeWe was elegant like Bergdorf Goodman or Saks Fifth Avenue. Had it really been so posh, or had I blown it all out of proportion? After all, I was dealing with the perception of what is beautiful to a ten-year-old.

I became interested in walking the wide, tree lined, clean streets, particularly after I recognized the prestigious boulevards. Yes, I was waking up from a long sleep. Alexander Platz, Brandenburger Tor, Unter den Linden, Kurfurstendam, and many more were important landmarks that I remembered. And they were still here. It was difficult to realize so many years had gone by . . . the Holocaust . . . WW II . . . all now history. I must be getting old, but . . .

<hr />

That evening Susie and I were waiting for Ati outside of our hotel. As her car approached the entrance I saw her wonderful beaming face, glowing with happiness through the car window. Ati hopped out, and embraced us. They hadn't seen each other in fifteen years, but it didn't matter . . . it felt like a few yesterdays ago. The mini tour tonight would whet our appetite. Each evening we would tell Ati what we had seen during the day, which places we would like to revisit, and she would take it from there.

Our hotel served an extensive buffet breakfast, but it was the roll-mops that caught my attention. Roll-mops are marinated filet of herring laid flat with thinly sliced onions and sour pickles, then rolled up and secured with a toothpick. I knew I was considered a big girl when I was served a whole one . . . just for me. For sixty years I have been thinking about that unique taste. Twice I found it in the US, but each time I was disappointed. Finally, it was in front of me . . . I was hesitant . . . reluctant to take the first bite. Very slowly I cut a piece . . . bit into it . . . it was good . . . but not great. In many ways I have changed in sixty years and probably so had my taste.

Our well-informed Protokoll tour guide had a pleasant manner, and spoke perfect English. The first day she pointed out some of the sights of Berlin that were important when I was a child: Die Siege Saule (the Golden Ilse Wings of Freedom) The Berlin Dom, Lustgarten, Brandenburger Tor, and the Tiergarten, similar to Central Park in New York . . . and more to come.

Bayerischer Platz had been a unique neighborhood when I lived there. I remember a small innocent looking community park with lovely landscaping and seating. What made this park outstanding today were the few brightly red painted benches. In the late 1930s, these were the only seats Jews were permitted to sit on. There is a plaque stating that Jews were only allowed to shop in certain grocery stores between 4-6 P.M. on Wednesday. Jews were forbidden to play any music, and by 1941 Jews were not able to leave the country or engage in any business. This memorial park was funded by a group of Berlin's German youths. It is encouraging that today's young are not ignoring their horrific history.

At one point of our tour I became uncomfortable. Our guide instructed the bus driver to stop in front of a castle. He parked the vehicle; a moment later a policeman appeared at his window and spoke defiantly to the driver. Our guide immediately exited the bus, approached the officer and a heated argument took place, which we couldn't hear. Viewing this situation, my imagination took over. I put a Nazi uniform on the policeman and suddenly I was back in 1938 Berlin. Was he a remnant of those days? Horrors. Our escort returned and stated that the officer was just flexing his muscles. I'm so grateful that Susie was with me. With incidents like this she will understand my abhorrence of uniforms.

That episode brought back another memory. Like all his young friends, Jeffrey wanted to become a Cub Scout. I, the good mother, took him to his first meeting and immediately took a dislike to the scout leader. He acted like he was God, shouted orders like the Nazis, and told the kids the importance of the uniform. I permitted Jeffrey to join . . . with a caveat . . . I refused to be a den mother. Al and I discussed my phobia . . . he understood and volunteered to be a den father. When Susie, three years later, wanted to be a Brownie, Al graciously took my place again. It didn't last long . . . thank goodness . . . Susie didn't like the brown uniform. I tried to explain my aversion about uniforms to my children.

At the present time Berlin's population is 3.5 million, compared to 4.5 million before WW II. In 1948 the Allied occupation consisting of Russia, France, England and the US divided Berlin. The Wall went up overnight in 1961.

It divided East Berlin from the West; the East being ruled by the Communists. During the twenty-eight years of Communist occupation, the German people who in the past had been hard working became lethargic. Overnight families and friends were separated for almost three decades. There was segregation, careers destroyed, and ambitions and hopes ruined. I felt sorry for the dilemma. Yes, the Berliners suffered when the Wall went up, but no one used them for medical experiments or put them in the ovens, as was done to Jews during Hitler's administration.

In 1989 the Wall came down and the total structure of Berlin changed again. The Berliners in the West looked down on their Eastern brothers.

Their communist work ethics, learned during the twenty-eight years of rule, was conflicting and caused strife. The Eastern sector had been neglected by esthetics. The Communist architecture was massive, gray, unimaginative, ugly, and badly constructed. Therefore, the decayed city was drab, devoid of trees and parks.

The majority of the houses were built in 1953 with Meissin tiles on the exterior. Most had fallen off, revealing asbestos, which had to be replaced at a tremendous expense. The West Berliners were angry at the tremendous cost of the unification, which changed the German economy significantly in the last years.

The enormous amount of construction in the East was immediately obvious. Cranes, cranes, and more cranes . . . everywhere. The colorful cranes represented the future of Berlin. One evening they were all lit in a variety of colors and choreographed to move for a production of The Dance of the Cranes. It was brilliant.

In 2000, Berlin would once again become the capital of Germany. Much of the construction consisted of building new embassies, representing dozens of countries, including ours. Museums and theaters were planned . . . Mercedes Benz and Sony invested billions of dollars. Berliners, in good times, loved their city and were now once again excited about its future.

Our next stop was the Plotzensee Memorial Center. The building had been a prison since 1879. More than 2,500 people were murdered there between 1933-1945. They came from a variety of social classes; religious, political, gypsies, homosexuals and ideological orientations. These people had been judged to be enemies of the German State.

Communists and Social Democrats were the first victims. Death by beheading or hanging was the merciless procedure. A failed attempt at assassinating Hitler took place July 20,1944. Subsequently 1,000 people were rounded up and executed at Plotzensee. They were hanged on butcher hooks. Hitler ordered camera teams to film their agony. Executions took place continuously until April 25,1945 when Russian troops occupied the prisons, and liberated the inmates.

Five butcher hooks remain as a reminder of the torture. An urn with soil and ashes from the concentration camp victims had been placed in front of the prison entrance as a memorial.

The streets of Berlin were quiet, clean and busy. Traffic was dense but kept moving. The people were well-behaved. Germans have a reputation for always obeying authority. *Maybe that was their undoing during the Hitler era.*

Our entire group went to City Hall for a formal welcome. A choir of school children greeted us when we entered the imposing building. They commenced to sing songs of my youth. Looking at the facial expression of my assemblage, I sensed their feeling of nostalgia. I didn't remember any of the songs, and concluded that I had blocked them out of my memory. I stood there and watched these good-looking youngsters, blond and blue eyed, singing to me. Was I hearing the German Youth Bund Choir of long ago? Will everything on this trip make me tremble? Did I make a mistake in coming back to Berlin? I'm grateful that Susie is standing next to me . . . without her at my side . . . I would have escaped.

We were ushered into an impressive salon. There, Mayor Eberhard Diepjen greeted us with a speech that set the tone for our visit. He stated that Protokoll was aware how difficult it must have been for some of us to come back to Berlin. He recognized that all of us were very young when we left under horrific circumstances. Mr. Diepjen, an attractive man in his fifties, stated, "We mourn for the members of your families and friends who didn't survive. There will be ghosts." He emphasized that what had happened was outrageous and must never happen again. The mayor spoke well, and was very sympathetic.

When the formalities were over, we gathered into small groups. I joined a circle of people and the Mayor, and in German told him that as soon as I had learned English

I never spoke my mother tongue to anyone again . . . including my parents . . . because of my anger toward anything German. With that said, I continued that I had been reluctant to come to Berlin but that my daughter persuaded me to do so. I introduced Susie to him, and then informed him that she doesn't understand German because I never wanted to teach it to my children. He immediately spoke English and remarked that it was feelings like mine that made his program important. From then on only English was spoken.

Immediately after I spoke to Mr. Diepjen two things happened. First: A woman, Susie's age, thanked me for verbalizing to the Mayor . . . exactly what her mother had been unable to say all these years. My statement made her finally understand her mother's behavior. Second: All the Protokoll personnel switched to English. None of the employees were Jewish, but all were dedicated to the pursuit of a better understanding.

In order for the 160 of us to meet, we were invited to a sumptuous buffet luncheon in another hall. Susie and I spoke to several interesting couples from Argentina, France and Australia, all spoke English. A ninety-year-old woman, who made this physically exhausting and traumatic journey, impressed me. And an eighty-year old man, who could have passed for George Burns with his looks, sense of humor and the ever—present cigar, amused me. When we returned to our hotel room, I fell into bed emotionally exhausted and fell asleep . . . and so did Susie.

In the evening Ati picked us up for some "serious" sightseeing. Her plan was to show us new places or return to places of particular interest that we had seen on our bus journey.

One of the outstanding sights of Berlin was THE WALL. I congratulate the Berliners for saving part of it as a memorial. Artists of all talents painted incredible images and collages on the panels. Most of the subject matter was political and angry. Much of it was done in cartoon form, some humorous and some brutally biting. Every board told a story. The most outstanding one was, "The Kiss," depicting Honiker, of Germany and Bresnev, of Russia, sealing a deal with a kiss. The artwork had been quickly executed, mostly unsigned, since the artists were fearful of being arrested for their political expression. It was a marvelous emotional history lesson through spontaneous art, in the street for all to see.

We went in and out of the Ati's car continuously looking at sights. She was determined for us not to miss anything. Susie and I had learned our lesson well . . . we immediately recognized East Berlin when Ati drove us there. "You are great students," she praised us.

No other city in the world ever had so much renovation, restoration and new construction planned in a two-year time frame. The new embassies are to be built in the East, where the Reichstag will have the place of honor. Brandenburger Tor and Unter den Linden had been the most prestigious landmarks for decades until their decline during WWII. All would be revitalized and once again become the showplace of Berlin. Everything was happening at a fever pitch. I felt the energy. Driving a car in the city was a trying experience due to the construction. Over all, the Berliners didn't complain . . . they understood the net result.

Ati had discovered a food market in East Berlin that specialized in meats, raw and cooked fish, salads and pickles. Susie and I were impressed. We had never seen such a variety of sour, garlic, half and half, very sour and spicy pickles. I was reminded of my childhood in the Lower East Side of New York, and the famous Pickle Man on Hester Street. He sold pickles out of the barrel . . . the ones on the bottom were always the best. Mr. Perlmutter had rolled up the sleeves of his white shirt, but they got juicy from the brine anyway. (Oh, how his armpits must have smelled!) He bellowed in front of his store; "A shtikel pickle for a nickel." My mother always bought one for me. I loved the very firm ones because with the first bite I heard a snap, and then the juices ran down my arm, and my eyes sparkled with happiness. It was glorious.

In the Berlin emporium there were more choices of pickles than at Mr. Perlmutter's store on Hester Street. "Let's go through them all until our stomachs ache," I suggested to Susie. She laughed. We hit the winner right away. I wasn't surprised at our talent . . . after all . . . we were New York City sour pickle mavens (connoisseurs).

Susie took the very sour, and I, the garlic. After only one bite, Susie crunched up her face, her eyes gleamed and she announced for all the Berliners to hear, "I can't believe it, Mom, this pickle is even better then Baba Lillie's."

That was quite a statement. She had loved my mother-in-law's specialty so much that she named her first cat Pickles. Since we couldn't finish the large converted cucumber, and Ati was ready to show us some more outstanding place, we wrapped the remains in wax paper, and brought our treasure into the car, to finish at a later time.

"Ladies . . . finish it NOW!" Ati begged. "The whole car smells of garlic."

We forced ourselves to do so . . . and smiled.

Whenever our group gathered, we asked each other questions in the hopes of making contacts from the past. One woman found a classmate who she hadn't seen since she was seven-years-old. From that moment on their eyes twinkled as they held hands, giggled like the schoolgirls they had been, and refreshed each other's memories with stories of long ago.

Another incident occurred at the bank. A woman in line wished to cash a check; the teller needed to verify the signature and asked her name. After the transaction was completed, a person on the same line approached the tourist, excused herself, and asked several questions. They soon discovered that they were cousins . . . both lived in Manhattan . . . only three blocks from each other. For sixty years each had thought that the other had died.

I was impressed with the many museums, especially the New National Gallery. It is an imposing modern building with exterior mustard colored wood panels that were designed by Van Mies. Seeing paintings by Kandinsky, Egon Schiele, Delauny, and Grabriele Munter, of the Red Rider period, popular in the 1920s, fascinated me. George Grosz, Max Ernst, and Kurt Schwitters represented the

Dada style. The sculpture garden, with a magnificent Henry Moore, was reminiscent of one at the MoMA in New York.

The tour bus picked us up for the night's entertainment at the Komischer Opera's performance of Don Giovanni. Susie and I dressed for the occasion in our New York sophisticated black. We fit right in with the Berliners, who favor dark clothing. The building was an impressive old opera house. The exterior was rococo, the interior, wine colored velvet with opulent Austrian crystal chandeliers. To our surprise, and disappointment, the Italian opera was sung in German. My expectations were shattered. The male voices were weak and the female's only a notch better. However, the sets were first-rate, imaginative, with huge minimalist columns, and unique lighting effects.

Could this be so? . . . I realized I dreamed in German!

The day was perfect for a sail on Havel Lake, in Wansee. The weather was clear, mild . . . perfect for a three hour chartered boat outing, in the suburb of Berlin. The excursion gave us another opportunity to befriend more of the people in the group.

I recalled to Susie that my family went to Wansee several times a year, and that I remembered the beautiful crystal clear lake, the sailboats, and especially the swans. There were lovely houses along the shoreline. Most of them appeared to be in excellent condition, built before WWII. I wondered, how many had belonged to Jews . . . and to whom do they belong now?

I had a strange feeling on the boat. Had I been here before? I knew the answer but I was looking for a flashback . . . like in the movies . . . seeing myself as the cute six-year-old, wearing her pretty hand-embroidered red dress, sitting and smiling on her father's lap, surrounded by a large group of happy relatives and friends. I treasure the photograph of that scene, but sadly there are only two of us in the photo who are still alive.

Martina Michels, Vice President of Abgeordneterhauses auf Berlin, (people who were forced to leave their homes for political reasons) was a very impressive speaker. In her thirties, not Jewish, the mother of two young children, she stated that she admired us for making this trip, knowing how traumatic the experience must be. The organization hoped that we would find a New Berlin, not the one we remembered.

"That is not to say that we should forget the past. The Holocaust must be remembered in order for it to never happen again," Martina emphasized.

Her task, and that of all Germans, particularly the children, was to understand their history, no matter how horrific. Mrs. Michels felt in order to be free, the question had to be addressed. She mentioned that many of the elderly didn't want to discuss the past.

"Of course not. What grandfather when asked by a grandchild, 'Opa, what did you do between 1933 to 1945?' would be able to answer honestly, 'I was in the SS and killed Jews.'"

The questions were difficult and rife with guilt. Martina reiterated that the point must be dealt with. German schoolbooks teach about the Holocaust in depth to this new generation. We in the US should do the same.

I totally agreed with her. People like me need to open their minds to the young Germans. They are innocent of the participation of the Holocaust, just as I am blameless concerning slavery and the injustices to the Blacks and Native Americans in our country.

———

Many people on the trip knew the complete address where they had lived. I remembered only the street name, Schoenhauser Allee. It is strange that I recall my Berlin telephone number, but in my head the digits are in German. As time passed, there is no one left who can answer my questions. I'm the matriarch now.

After a day or two, I really felt that I had walked these streets ages ago. It was on a stroll that I thought of lovable Ella, our maid, who always held my hand when we walked in the neighborhood, and when she took me to school. My family loved her. Now I wonder . . . what happened to Ella? Did she marry and have children?? Did she remember that we, a Jewish family, loved her? And did she have fond thoughts of us? If she married, was her husband a Nazi? I hope she had a good life . . . she was good to me.

Slowly I came out of my trance and started to recognize street names. I felt excitement. Ati wasn't surprised that she hadn't recognized some of the names. When the Wall went up, the Communists changed many street names of the formerly famous names to sound more Russian. Three decades later when the Wall came down, the West Berlin government went in the opposite direction and changed Chekhovstrasse to a more generic German name.

Ati, our fabulous tour guide, drove us to Postsdam, in the outskirts of Berlin. That city became known after WWII when the Allies signed the Potsdam Agreement, which gave the military rights to the four victorious countries: Russia, France, Great Britain and the United States.

It is a lovely peaceful suburban town with sparkling lakes and rivers where Albert Einstein had his summerhouse, before he emigrated to Princeton, N.J. in 1935. His simple cottage is now a museum.

The day was full of points of interest. When we had lunch at a lakeside restaurant I became aware that the little German children were absolutely beautiful and well-behaved. They all seemed to have magnificent large blue eyes, extraordinary blond, almost white hair, and rosy apple cheeks. The atmosphere felt like a fairy tale. For several moments this image really unnerved me. Everything was so perfect . . . the children looked like painted dolls. Time stood still, and I thought, *Had there ever been a war . . . or a Holocaust here?*

I had a special request . . . I wanted to visit a site that was not on the tour . . . the Berlin train station where Ruthchen and I, as ten-year-old best girlfriends, said a tearful *Auf Wiedersehen*, in 1938. We were strong, naïve, but most of all obedient children. My imagination transported me to that station platform. I saw us as though I were watching a film clip of my life from sixty years ago. Ruth constantly was on my mind; it made me both happy and sad.

Returning to Berlin in the evening took longer than anticipated due to detours caused by the massive construction. For Ati, this was no problem . . . she just found more things for us to look at. We passed an area of houses that had been abandoned. These buildings had changed ownership numerous times since the 1930s.

Many had probably belonged to Jews, then Germans, and eventually were occupied by Russia. The houses cannot be rented or sold due to litigation. The question is: Who are the rightful owners? It is a difficult political problem.

After fourteen hours of touring we were back in Berlin. It was late but Ati had planned to take us to a restaurant that was famous for its New York cheese blintzes. Ati thinks of everything. She drove for an hour without success looking for a parking spot . . . NYC, revisited. At past ten o'clock we thanked her for an outstanding day. Ati was disappointed . . . she wanted to go on . . . we didn't let her . . . she had work the next day. We hugged and thanked her when she left us off in front of our hotel. As soon as Susie and I entered the lobby, we knowingly looked at each other, turned around, left the hotel and found a Chinese restaurant one street corner away. We had a giggle about that. We can stay up late, take naps at any time, eat at any hour, but the truth . . . the food was very ordinary. This was certainly not Chinatown. However, it had been a marvelous fourth day.

In the 1930s there were 500,000 Jews living in Germany; 180,000 resided in Berlin. Jews had been an integral part of Germany going back to the thirteenth century. A documented letter exists written by Mr. Wallenwebern in 1295, mentioning a Jew with whom he had business connections. Records confirm that Jews have lived in Berlin since 1671. That information makes me understand why many Jews, whose ancestors had lived in Germany for generations, even centuries, had such loyalty to their country. They were naïve to believe that with that history they would be safe from Hitler's tyranny. My ancestors were not born in Germany and had no ties there, and not to Austria-Hungry, either, which became Poland after WWI.

Today Germany has a population of eighty million, with only 40,000 Jews, 10,000 living in Berlin. Most are recent immigrants from Russia. When I lived there as a child, there were FORTY-SIX synagogues in Berlin, today there are FOUR.

The next day's stop was Die Neue Synagogue built in 1856. A benefit concert for the Jewish Organization took place there in 1930, with Albert Einstein as the violin soloist.

I was thrilled . . . this was the orthodox synagogue where my parents were married, my brother a Bar Mitzvah, and to which my grandparents donated a Torah. As a child I thought this temple to be the most beautiful. But even at such a young age, I thought it unfair that the men and women were segregated, instead of being on banquettes together as a family . . . the men had seats downstairs and the women in the balcony.

My mother and grandmother had a bench in the first row mezzanine where I was able to look down and see my papa, brother, and grandfather. I always waited patiently for my father to look up, to the balcony. The custom was for the women to mix raisins and nuts, put them into small brown paper bags, and throw the goodies down for the Bar Mitzvah boy and his friends.

Those were happy days for all of us, surrounded by our loved ones. I have been seeking another synagogue as beautiful that could give me the peace and comfort of the Neue Synagogue. I have not found one yet.

On that quest I thought, is this just a little girl's perception of beauty, or did it really exist?

In Berlin I found the answer.

The Wehrmacht took this magnificent building on Kristallnacht, November 1, 1938. (My immediate family left six months before.) When the Allies bombed Berlin several years later, the temple was severely damaged. After the war the synagogue was returned to the Jewish Organization, however, all that remained of its magnificence was the front entrance wall.

Renovations are now in progress. The original architectural plans have been found. When our group entered the house of worship, I immediately saw a gigantic blow-up photo of the interior of the sanctuary, showing the male congregation at prayer. I strained my eyes to find my grandfather in the group . . . without success. The beauty of the synagogue overwhelmed me. My heart beat fast and warm tears trickled down my cheeks. I was grateful that my memory hadn't deceived me. The photo and the place were just as I remembered it . . . sixty years ago.

A large hallway was temporarily used as a museum that houses bits and pieces of salvaged Judaic artifacts . . . each object precious. The tour was full of anguish, but at the same time it was a gratifying experience that I will carry in my heart forever. Each day Susie learns more about my past.

All 160 members of our group entered the makeshift sanctuary of the synagogue, where Mr. Landsman spoke to us. He introduced himself: His parents married in the early 1930s, in Berlin, and he was born soon after. Mr. Landsman's father was Jewish and his mother a Christian, who converted to Judaism. The Nazis invaded his home one night and dragged his father out. He ended up in Shanghai. The little boy and his mother somehow survived the terrible war years in Berlin. He never saw his father again; he died of tuberculosis in Shanghai. Mr. Landsman has lived in Berlin his whole life and has totally dedicated himself to restoring the synagogue.

His was a very dramatic story, which intensified when a man in our group suddenly stood up, interrupted, "Excuse me, I can't contain myself any longer . . . was your father Morris Landsman?"

"Yes."

"Mr. Landsman . . . I knew your father."

His statement was electrifying. A hush came over the sanctuary. Everyone seemed to hold their breath . . . wanting to hear more. Mr. Landsman's face lost all color. The American explained that he with his parents and brother were also shipped to Shanghai . . . where his father contracted TB . . . as did Mr. Landsman . . . and was hospitalized. The two young fathers had beds next to each other and became friends. The little boy visited as often as possible. The senior Mr. Landsman must have cherished those visits as well since his son, in Berlin, was the same age. As sad as that story was, Mr. Landsman was happy to get additional information about his papa.

It's hard to rationalize about these encounters . . . they were happy and they were sad . . . but I believe it was all good for the soul. We were not ashamed of our cascading tears. At times it was emotionally exhausting . . . I needed to escape by taking a nap.

Every encounter was special in some way. The bus took us to Auguststrasse where Ruthchen and I met and went to school. From kindergarten until we said goodbye to each other, five years later, we were inseparable and always sat next to each other.

The building no longer exists and in its place is a Home for the Aged. In reality, Ruth and I have traveled from youth to senior age as well.

Today was the most traumatic of the trip, so far. The first stop was the Gedentafel at Levetszowstrasse. The pogrom started here during Kristallnacht in November 1938. It was one of the most outrageous displays of Nazi barbarism in Berlin. A quiet residential neighborhood where 200,000 lived in apartment houses was chosen as a collection depot. Jews were gathered from their homes in the middle of the night, and then shipped to Auschwitz, and certain death. The Nazis were proud of their precise record keeping. The gigantic steel plaque lists the dates, railroad car serial numbers, the total of people picked up each day, and locations where they were transported to. On some days there were as many as 1,500 victims. It is unconscionable to imagine the joy the Gestapo must have derived from their precise bookkeeping records.

On another site there were gigantic marble tablets representing the forty-six synagogues that were in Berlin during that time. One huge stone sculpture, larger than life, simulated a boxcar with hordes of people herded together with no space to sit or breath, and bound with heavy wire cord.

Another was a modern concept of a railroad car with no windows, used to ship the thousands of Jews to extermination. The impact of viewing these pieces of "art" was indescribable. The Germans of today want this reminder.

On the way back to our hotel the bus stopped at an overpass. Looking at the train trestle below, one could see a large sculpture of the Star of David perched on a staircase . . . going to nowhere. It is a daily reminder to humanity that the railcars on the tracks below hauled Jews to concentration camps.

Proving that anti-Semitism is not dead, the sculpture was vandalized in a middle of the night. The Berlin government immediately rebuilt it. There was no repeat performance . . . a lesson learned?

It had been an emotional exhausting day, but it was not over yet. Ati was making a birthday party for me in the evening. Her timing was perfect; Susie and I needed a change of atmosphere. My dear friend, and her husband, Peter, invited sixteen friends to their home. The table was beautifully set for a scrumptious buffet dinner that Ati cooked completely herself. The menu literally went from soup (wild mushroom) to nuts, including a Sacha Torte, wines, champagne and flowers . . . everywhere.

But the best part of all was the stimulating conversations that evening with their intelligent, aware, liberal-minded friends. Everyone spoke perfect English; there was lots of laughter, and good humor. Susie became involved in a conversation with a woman in her fifties, who expounded that she had a difficult time dealing with the fact that both of her parents were Nazis.

I was introduced to a woman who had emigrated from Russia six years ago. She related that in Russia she had concealed that she was Jewish, and now in Berlin, she felt completely free about her religious preference. I was astounded and happy.

At some point during the evening I was asked about my recent experiences in Berlin. I truthfully was able to say that I was impressed with the honesty and goals of some of the German people. Each day I became more comfortable . . . but not completely. It was a memorable 70th birthday party in my honor by an outstanding friend, in the city where I was born. The realization felt strange. I capped the evening by announcing: "I'm a new-old-Berliner."

September 15, 1997

Seventy years ago I was born here . . . in Berlin. Just to recognize that fact felt strange.

I was completely surprised when I entered the hotel dining room for breakfast and was greeted by Mr. Nemitz, extending a hand toward me and congratulating me on my birthday. As a token, he presented me with a porcelain bowl, inscribed from Berlin. To be remembered so far from home felt good . . . but in Berlin? It felt strange . . . I couldn't come to terms with the truth . . . I actually lived here for the first ten years of my life. Today I'm so far from home . . . miles away . . . an ocean apart. I felt like a tourist . . . and I was . . . So What's The Big Deal? Here where I stand is where I was born, but my allegiance is to my adopted country. America . . . Miss Liberty . . . she took me in . . . I LOVE YOU.

It all seemed so unreal, so strange . . . hard to believe. I've come full circle. Birthdays had never been very important to me but today felt unique . . . was I acting on stage . . . was I supposed to feel that I belong? If I'd come on this trip alone . . . I might have felt . . . I don't know . . . sad . . . abandoned . . . but Susie was with me . . . it was okay.

At noon the touring bus took us to the Opernpalais, a beautiful palace at Unter den Linden, for a farewell brunch where all 160 of us would meet for the last time. As Susie and I stepped off the bus, Mr. Nemitz approached me with a big smile, gallantly took my arm in his, (Europeans do that so well) and escorted me to the table of honor in the Prinzessinnen Saal. He made a big deal because it was my birthday. (Again? I thought we were finished with that.) The Saal was a grand, beautiful ballroom. Round tables, seating eight, with beautiful china and silver place settings, and a magnificent crystal bowl of roses, in various pinks and peach, and interspersed with baby's breath placed at the center.

Mr. Nemitz introduced me to two guests of honor. At my right; Dr. Bernard Fisher, the head of Protokoll in Berlin; to my left, Dr. Herman Simon, Director of Judaicum of Berlin, and the New Synagogue. I was totally unprepared for this attention. My cheeks flushed. The other four guests, besides Susie and me, were Dr. Waltraud Rehfeld, a former Resistance Fighter, a journalist stationed in London, the assistance to Dr. Fisher, and Mrs. Levine.

Mrs. Levine's story was intriguing. Mrs. Levine too had been born in Berlin, and emigrated to Argentina with her husband and two small children in the 1930s. Her family lived there until 1961 when they returned to Berlin. Her husband went into business and became wealthy. Now a widow, she has been the supporting rock for Jewish causes, and particularly for the New Synagogue.

I had the opportunity to ask her, "Wasn't it difficult for you to come back to Berlin in '61, not long after the Holocaust?"

She gave me a knowing look and answered, "We do what we have to do." It is hard for me to imagine making such a choice.

Both Drs. Simon and Fisher spoke eloquently, and mentioned that we probably had seen ghosts from our past, just as the Mayor of Berlin had mentioned the first day after we arrived. With that statement I thought of my beautiful Opa Jacob, (grandfather) who looked like Theodore Hertzl, (founder of Zionism) tall, with deep blue eyes and a long well-groomed red beard. It was he and my Oma who donated the Torah to the synagogue. He died suddenly when I was seven, and I was devastated. I missed sitting on his lap, and sucking the rock candy that he always had in his vest pocket . . . whispered that it was just for me . . . it was our secret. Even now I can still recall how his breath smelled of sweets. Luckily he died in his own bed, not in a concentration camp. He was a good ghost.

Dr. Fisher reminded us that the purpose of this trip was for us to come to terms with some of the ghosts. The organization's hope was that in these few days we had been somewhat educated to make us less bitter and more forgiving.

Dr. Simon told of his background. He too had been born in Berlin. His parents met in the 1930s. Being a dedicated Zionist, his father went to Palestine, while his mother stayed behind. After the war he returned and looked for his sweetheart, and miraculously found her. His father wished to take her back to Palestine. She refused. He married her, and remained in Berlin. The war years in Berlin must have been horrendous for a young Jewish woman trying to survive.

I listened to his story intently and then said, "Dr. Simon, your mother must have some unbelievable stories to tell." He sadly stated that his mother never talked of those years. The guilt of having survived prevented some people from speaking. In some cases it paralyzed persons for life. Dr. Simon believed that without letting go, the healing could never take place. His devotion to his mother made this program very important to him.

After the sumptuous buffet, Susie got into conversation with a woman from Fairfield, Connecticut, whose husband also was born in Berlin and was my age. I was introduced, and Sig's wife immediately questioned me: What city did I move to when I arrived in the US . . . what was my maiden name . . . what year did I arrive in the States? My maiden name didn't interest her, but the fact that I moved to Bridgeport did. She felt deeply about her husband being connected to me in some way. Her questioning continued. I had a premonition that an important unknown was about to occur. Although all my answers were negative, Sig's wife did not relent. The interrogation continued. When she asked what my mother's maiden name was. "Wolf," I answered . . . her eyes lit up. Sig was getting annoyed with her persistence and told her to stop.

"Helga said 'Wolf'"

"Wolf is a common name," Sig snapped at her.

At that point she really pressed on. Her husband became irritated with her, at which point she gave him a look that conveyed . . . if you don't let me continue, you're going to be in trouble with me.

He shrugged his shoulders in resignation and asked me, "Do you happen to know a Morris Wolf?"

"Of course . . . he's my uncle."

There was complete astonishment . . . a look of disbelief on Sig's face.

"Oh, my god . . . your uncle sponsored me and two of my cousins to the United States. He saved our lives!"

I was thrilled. For the moment we were all speechless. Sig told us part of his story. He was an only child, and remained in Berlin until 1941. When he was thirteen, he luckily got out of Germany on the last Kinderbot to England. Thousands of Jewish parents made the most horrible, heart-wrenching decisions of their lives, and sent their children away as a last resort to save them from extermination. Those who were sent to England were the most fortunate.

Sig was lucky in one respect, he eventually got to America, but his parents didn't. They waited in Berlin for exit visas that arrived too late. His mother and father were arrested and shipped to Auschwitz where they both died. The most treasured possession Sig has were several letters from his father telling him that he loved him, and to be patient.

Through Morris Wolf's sponsorship, Sig lived with an uncle in Bridgeport. This was an amazing coincidence. As excited as a little child, he recited all my cousins', aunts', and uncles' names. He knew them all. Sig mentioned that he was friends with my cousin, George; Morris Wolf's son.

I felt proud of my uncle. Susie was amazed. For years she had heard me tell about Uncle Morris . . . about his sponsoring over a hundred people to the United States, most of whom he never knew. Here was positive proof of my uncle's humanitarian generosity.

Sig and I were on a tremendous emotional high. There was so much to talk about. We decided to meet for dinner and continue. Sitting across the table at the restaurant we continued the repartee, and caught up with old times. Sig had the feeling that our paths had crossed when we were young children in Berlin. He knew all my cousins who had lived in the same large apartment house, as my grandparents. His theory made sense; if he played with my cousins in my grandparents' house, then I must have been there many times too. I was too young to be interested in boys; I didn't remember him.

Finally we ran out of questions, or so we thought. This time it was my gut feeling that pushed me to question Sig.

"Did you know Ruth Scherzer?"

His face suddenly twitched . . . his eyes bulged and for a few moments his mouth stayed open . . . no sound emerged. Was he having a stroke?

The Ruth in question was of course my best friend. She was the only one who had been permitted to come to the Berlin train station to say goodbye to me in 1938. When Sig got his wind back, he told me that he had wanted to question me about Ruth, but felt it was too far-fetched. His wife had come over to our table when suddenly he couldn't contain himself any longer and announced:

"I've been in love with her since I was nine! She was so beautiful," he whispered breathlessly, gazing up to the sky, as if he were thinking of an angel.

We all laughed. I couldn't believe it. Imagine . . . after all these years . . . I found a secret. What fun Ruth and I would have had, had we known about Sig's feelings? I smiled, imagining the giggling and teasing that would have taken place between two nine-year-old girls. Sig had been in love with Ruthchen. I filled him in about his long lost loves past sixty years.

I called Ruth in Chile as soon as I returned to the States. She vaguely remembered Sig, and laughed it off.

We left the restaurant. Ten of us congregated in the street not wanting to say good night . . . it was our last chance to commiserate . . . we were leaving in the morning. Sig excitedly told of our connection. And then a woman from California told about her life in Shanghai during the war. She related of having been in a slave labor camp for years with her parents. Even the youngest children were expected to work, getting just enough food to survive. The redeeming feature was that the families remained together.

As she continued her story, mention was made that her husband, Jack, had also been in Shanghai as a young boy; however, they met as adults many years later in California. The wife noted that Jack was a classical musician. I wanted to know where and whether he was still performing.

"Yes, he played for the Opera, in New York."

I turned to Jack, who just joined our group, "Jack, did you know Aaron Shapinsky?"

"Did I know him?" Jack exclaimed. "I played with him for thirty years . . . I loved that man!"

Aaron was my husband's first cousin, and Susie's second cousin. I had fun relating outrageously humorous stories about a very wonderful, eccentric talented family of musicians and a painter. Each tale reminded me of another. I had an attentive audience and Susie was able to hear these scenarios about her cousins again.

For two hours we stood in the street in Berlin, reminisced and laughed. It was 1997. If we had done the same in 1938, we would have been arrested.

The following day it was time to bid farewell. We had breakfast with Ati and Peter. The four of us hugged in a warm embrace, and said a reluctant *Auf Wiedersehen.* Years pass between our visits, but when we meet, it feels like a continuation of when we left off. I treasure such friendship, and I have the same with Ruthchen.

I have come full circle.

Epilogue

How was the trip?
Are you glad that you went?
Would you go back to Berlin . . . to Germany?
Would you consider living there?

These were the questions brought to my attention. It was an unbelievable trip of a lifetime. It was emotionally exhausting, informative, optimistic, unique, sad, and happy. I missed Ruthchen and thought about her constantly. It would have been fascinating to hear our different thoughts and opinions when visiting the places we remembered from our childhood.

I learned about today's German youth and pitied the guilt they have when thinking of what some of their ancestors are responsible for. I'm grateful that Susie persuaded me to make the trip, and that she was my support. I learned much about myself. I actually enjoyed speaking German and was amazed at how much I remembered.

Would I return to Berlin?

"Yes, and No." I would have no problem visiting Ati. Berlin is a fascinating city and there is more of interest that I would like to see.

Would I consider living there?

"No, No, No."

I have no allegiance to Germany. Sadly we cannot determine where we are born. If I had a choice, it would be . . . Greenwich Village, in New York.

The United States of America is my country. It is not the perfect place in today's cruel world; but it is the best for me.

———

Ruth (Ruthchen) died at eighty-two, in 2009. I surprised her with my trip to Chile, for her eightieth birthday party. We were friends for seventy-seven-years.

My Susie (Susan) died at fifty-four, in 2010. I'm forever grateful that we made the Berlin trip together.

I miss her terribly.

ALI, NAI NAI AND SUSIE

"I'm going to adopt a baby girl from China," Susie announced nonchalantly at an intimate dinner party in honor of my sixty-ninth birthday.

It's amazing how contained she was. Had it been me, I would have shouted the announcement to the world. I never dreamed of such birthday present . . . it really felt that it was a gift. Finally I was going to have a grandchild . . . a girl.

There was nothing that could have made me happier. When in her thirties, Susie talked about wanting a child. She was not married and thought about the possibility of in-vitro. Now that she was forty she decided not to wait for "Mr. Right." Her independent nature assured her that she could do it. Adoption.

Research informed her that China permitted single women to adopt . . . with no strings attached. I was thrilled and in total agreement.

The Talmud says:

A Mother is liken unto a
Mountain spring that nourishes

143

The tree at the root, but one
Who mothers another's child
Is likened unto a water
That rises into a cloud and
Goes a long distance to
Nourish a lone tree in the desert.

The Chinese government has a law . . . one child per family. Due to this ruling many girl babies (and handicapped boys) are abandoned by their biological parent. When found, the infants are immediately placed in orphanages and become the property of China. The security for the adoptive parent is solid. Once the paperwork is approved, and payment is made to China, the child is legally the adoptive parent's . . . for life.

Susie agreed to my joining her on this journey. The process was grueling, exhausting, and frustrating. The Chinese bureaucracy with its rigid rules and regulations, the unbelievable amount of paperwork, and the payment of monies to China took over a year. On one frightening occasion there was a two months' hold on adoption due to a British television report that maligned the Chinese government for inhumane conditions in some of the orphanages. We knew that it was important to not panic, and remain optimistic. It wasn't easy.

After a year, when all the documents were in order, we received a postage stamp size photo of the baby. We immediately fell in love with Ali Mao Yi Harris, who stared at us with intelligent, big, round, dark eyes. That first photo of Ali, named after my deceased husband, Al, changed the appearance of my refrigerator door forever. There are over a hundred photos on that door.

Receiving the final confirmation from our Sarasota social worker, who worked in consort with the orphanage in China, gave us a wonderful excuse to celebrate at a Chinese restaurant. Susie asked what name I would like to be called by Ali. I went through the usual litany . . . Grandma . . . Nana . . . Bubi . . . none of which seemed to fit my liking. "I'll ask the Chinese interpreter when we get there." There was lots of time to decide.

Our social worker informed us that by the time we pick Ali up, from the date that Susie started the process eighteen months ago; she would be almost seven months old. My daughter requested a child as young as possible. She felt that psychologically it would be best for the child. Ali's weight would be approximately twelve pounds . . . definitely below the norm. Not knowing if the child was on milk or lactose formula, we took both. Our luggage for the baby supplies became heavy . . . rice cereal, bottles, nipples, oils, shampoo, medications, lots of diapers and clothing. Purchasing adorable little girl outfits and cuddly toys was the highlight for me. Our personal needs were unimportant. Susie and I were picking up a baby, not being American tourists at the Ritz. Actually, the White Swan Hotel in Guangzhou (formally Canton) is a five star hotel. The orphanages had a reasonable deal with the hotel. On our return with Ali, after hopefully having secured her visa from the US Consulate, as well as the permit for her to leave China, we'd stay at the White Swan Hotel again.

We left Sarasota September 11, 1996. The itinerary: Sarasota, San Francisco, Taiwan, Hong Kong, Guangzhou, and finally, Maoming, China. On the flight to San Francisco, Susie was napping when I came across a very disturbing article in *The New York Times*. It stated that the previous day a typhoon had hit Maoming, the location of the orphanage where Ali lived. The report claimed that thirty-three people died, over sixteen hundred were injured, and three hundred thousand houses destroyed. Can that be possible? The paper further reported that there was no electricity . . . roads had been washed away . . . no telephone service was available. My pulse raced. I thought, *where is Ali? What happened to the orphanage, the hundred children, and the people who cared for them?* As Susie slept peacefully beside me, I wondered if I should tell her the grave news or keep the information to myself. She had the right to know.

I woke her. For the first time in forty-one years I saw my strong daughter become hysterical. Susie feared that with no water the formulas could not be prepared. With no communication what would we . . . could we do? I cradled my adult child in my arms. We cried together. Thirty-five thousand feet above the earth we wondered how this scenario would play out.

Susie used the Airphone to call our social worker in Sarasota, who was not aware of the situation in Maoming. Her advice was, "Proceed as planned. Special efforts probably will be made for the babies that are being adopted. The brick house they live in is large. Think positive."

146

The first stop was Hong Kong, where we made connections with four other families from the same American adoption agency. Throughout this voyage we stayed together in a group . . . stayed at the same hotels . . . ate all our meals together. We had Liz, our own Chinese social worker, and Ching; the interpreter whose English was flawless. The young women were always with us, and answered all our questions with patience and empathy.

"Ching, what is the Chinese word for grandmother?"

"Po Po," she answered. Susie and I laughed. In Yiddish that word means a person's behind. We explained our amusement . . . she giggled. Ching differentiated between Po Po, the word for the maternal grandmother, and Nai Nai, for the paternal grandfather. I loved the sound of Nai Nai, and looked at Susie who had a great smile on her face. We agreed. It's perfect. From now on I shall be known as Nai Nai to my granddaughter and her friends.

Every day of our journey was spent going to some Chinese government agency to sign papers and pay monies . . . in fresh new $100 bills. When still in the States, we were advised to bring only crisp new bills, and to be certain that the four corners were not bent! My bank had to order my request.

Besides being careful about the large amount of cash we all carried, which was nerve wracking, we also had to guard the dossier. If even only one of the many pages were missing, the whole transaction would be cancelled. Susie and I divided the dollars, and strapped it to different places on our bodies. The dossier never left Susie's body, even when she slept. We were warned not to trust the hotel vaults, and to take special care of our passports, as they were worth fifty thousand dollars on the black market. When waiting at bus and train stations, (we moved to several different cities to get documents signed) our luggage was tethered and watched by our group at all times.

On the fifteenth of September we were all dining at the White Swan Hotel, still childless, when I was presented with a luscious chocolate cake commemorating my birthday. I was greatly touched, but my mind was on getting Ali. It was getting closer to the time of our arrival at the orphanage. All of us were getting edgy.

On the nine-hour train trip to Maoming, an industrial city, I saw the terrain change from monotonous to grasslands, to awesome mountain ranges. Peering through the window I concluded that the farm population was poor, and the people toiled hard with outdated equipment. Every hour a uniformed person pushed food carts through the aisles. Ching was always with us to explain the menu. Except for noodles and rice the food didn't look like the Chinese fare we were accustomed to eating in the States. Susie and I liked the authentic Chinese food.

"Tomorrow, the seventeenth is THE DAY!" This was the long awaited announcement from Ching. Early in the morning, the five families, bleary eyed and disheveled, met for breakfast. We would be childless for the last time. Eating meals will be different from then on. A large comfortable van picked us up and drove us through the city. I didn't notice any remnants of the typhoon *The New York Times* had reported a week ago. I questioned Ching. She explained that this area was used to having hurricanes, and that the debris was quickly cleaned up. I found the statement interesting since the railroad, and bus stations, as well as the streets, were filthy, everywhere I'd been in China, not including the White Swan Hotel, of course.

All was quiet in the van. We were fantasizing. Finally we arrived at the orphanage and were quickly ushered into the substantial two-story brick building. I felt as if we were being sneaked in . . . to a conference room on the second floor. It was obvious that all the other areas were off-limits to us. My suspicion proved correct when Susie attempted to leave our group . . . to look around. My adventurous daughter was immediately detoured and returned to our group.

Once we were ushered into the room, the narrow door was kept closed. Tea was served. No one had any interest in it. We were waiting for the babies. There we sat . . . in a trance. Some of us paced the room . . . waiting . . . for the insignificant looking door to open. The babies would come through that opening that all of us were focused on. I must say we were an unattractive looking group . . . disheveled . . . bleary eyed . . . stressed out . . . exhausted. Any noise made us jump. Our nerves were frayed. I kept checking the time on my watch . . . absurd . . . what difference did it make? The right time would be when the door opened and the babies were placed into our arms.

The waiting was excruciating. What was holding up the process? Was there a glitch? Was this done on purpose? We were on time . . . as arranged . . . where were they?

The room was quiet. There was nothing to say. Small talk was superfluous. We all had the same thoughts. More than a half an hour had passed . . . waiting . . . and waiting . . . staring toward the closed door. My eyes felt strained and tired. That door . . . if only it opened.

To change my concentration I walked to the window and noticed a garden below. I smiled when I saw colorful clothing gently dancing in the hot breeze, suspended by wooden clothespins on the many wash-lines. The garments belonged to the hundred children living in the facility. But today was a special day . . . five babies would be leaving the orphanage and starting a new life.

My reality was that the door would open, our surnames would be called, and one by one, each caretaker would bring our precious baby to us. That would have been easy . . . but no . . . it wasn't to be simple. Instead all five custodians came through the door, almost simultaneously, and called out the Chinese names of our new daughters. When these abandoned babies were brought to the orphanage, they were given names . . . all starting with Mao . . . Mao Ye, Mao Yen, Mao Yi, Mao Deng and Mao Ying. It was terribly confusing. Did we hear correctly? The first two babies names were called. Susie kept starring. I was so intent on getting this momentous moment documented on the video camera. I was more a photographer than a participant. After all, Susie depended on me to get the first pictures of her daughter. It was now, or never. She had purchased the camcorder the day before we left on our trip, and I received my only lesson the night before. Total responsibility for filming our family history was mine.

When finally Mao Yi was announced, Susie hesitated. She needed to be certain that the baby she was handed was the correct one. When the name was called the second time, Susie looked at Ali's big round black eyes and she knew that this was the same face as on the tiny photo we had received three months ago. The caretaker came forward and placed Ali Mao Yi Harris into Susie's outstretched arms. In a melodic soft voice, with tears of joy trickling down her cheeks, the new mother sang out, "She's so beautiful . . . she's so beautiful."

The camera kept rolling until I could no longer contain myself. I placed the camcorder on a table, walked over to Susie, and wrapped my arms around my daughter, and granddaughter . . . kissed them both . . . cried from sheer ecstasy and relief. Ali's gaze was transfixed on us. She made no sound.

Susie lovingly placed the child into my arms. There was nothing, . . . absolutely nothing . . . more magical than that moment. I wanted time to stand still . . . to savor each precious second.

Over forty years ago when I saw my own two children for the first time, I was thrilled. But this situation was more emotional. It's impossible to explain the feeling. It was different . . . glorious . . . awesome . . . a revelation . . . more meaningful. Jeffrey and Susie understood my feelings when I explained it to them.

I kept thinking, *Susie saved the life of another mother's child.*

The five families huddled around each other, introduced the little girls to the new parents of their former crib mates. In the orphanage they usually slept two or three babies per crib . . . no wiggle room. We were all family now. Each of us looked thrilled with the gift that we had just received. All of us were part of a lottery. All winners.

My continuing question was, "Out of the one hundred children in this orphanage, (six months to fifteen years) how was Ali, and the rest, chosen to be adopted?" This child, who in the Chinese system would have been neglected, given a meager education, been doomed to life in the lowest rung of their society, had been chosen to join my loving family in Sarasota, Florida. With us she would get all the advantages for possible happiness, a good education, excellent medical treatment . . . and most importantly . . . lots of love. I wondered if it was sheer luck.

After tearful goodbyes to the caretakers, we were permitted to leave with our precious cargo. It felt strange. None of the babies cried when we were in the van. Why not? Suddenly after six months of their life, they were separated from the people they had known and recognized. Now there were in the arms of strangers, who spoke a strange sounding language, and probably smelled different as well.

We came empty to the orphanage, but each family left with a treasure.

Can we really keep Ali?

Is she really ours?

Forever?

These children were chosen for us . . . by what criteria? We asked Ching, but she had no answer. It was shocking to learn that the babies had never been out of the building since they were brought to the facility six months ago, all being about the same age . . . had never felt the fresh air on their little bodies. The explanation . . . the facility was under staffed. The goodbyes took a long time, or so it seemed. We had to be polite. Of course all of us wanted to get back to our respective hotel rooms and examine our babies. In the van there were now five infants as quiet as sleeping kittens. That was strange . . . almost dream-like.

When we got out of the hotel elevator, a servant with a shy smile greeted us. She bowed and quickly ran, holding a thermos of boiling water for the baby's formula to our room. Her noiseless little steps made me curious . . . *had her feet been bound?* She opened the door, placed the thermos on a platter, bowed again, smiled at Ali and promptly, without making a sound, quietly exited the room.

Maoming is an industrial city, in the Southwestern part of China, not on a tourist list of points of interest. The guests, except for the five American families, were all male businessmen, dressed in black slacks and white shirts . . . like a uniform. They knew why we were there. Frequently a guest or staff person would look at Ali and say, "Lucky baby. Lucky baby." They were all gracious, knowing that these were all girls, (no boys, unless disabled) leaving China for a new life in another country.

Finally in our hotel room, Susie kissed Ali's face and gently laid her on the bed. Mother and grandmother held hands and just stared at this new treasure that looked right back at us with wide, big, black eyes. She still made no sound. In the orphanage, no matter what the temperature, the babies were swaddled in lots of clothing, not for warmth, but for security. They slept two or three to a crib. Thus confined, the infants couldn't move much in any direction. Under those conditions it's easier for the meager staff to control the children.

Susie undressed Ali. First she removed the little white knit undershirt, and then the pink cotton, crudely hand sewn, pants. Ali was happy with the attention she was getting. To our surprise she was wearing a mustard colored piece of clothing instead of a diaper. The fabric was draped like a Jodhpur, and tied together with a torn strip of cloth. When removed we were astonished to see that it was an adult tee shirt! Susie and I were flabbergasted and agreed that we would leave some new baby clothes behind at the orphanage, and take these with us, as a keepsake.

The babies didn't wear diapers (too costly). When the infants were strong enough to sit up, they wore clothes with an opening on the bottom, and sat in a highchair with a potty underneath, for hours. The babies got no stimulation, become lethargic, and eventually fell asleep. Ten o'clock was the last feeding and no matter if the little ones cried, no one attended to them until six in the morning. At such an early age the babies learned that it is useless to fret . . . no one comes to their aid. That explains why the children were so quiet.

Upon examination we saw that little Ali was well formed, but small for her age. At almost seven months she weighed only twelve pounds. Her dexterity was not good. She was not able to hold her head up without assistance, nor hold the soft, plush little toys that the other babies in our group were able to manipulate.

Susie lifted Ali in the air, and a remarkable thing happened. She was nude and stretched her little arms way out, as if she had wings. Her little legs went into a complete split. Ali stayed in that position for quite a while, as if soaring. She was free at last . . . and loved it.

It is possible that when Ali and I took a bath together that first night, that it was her first time? Probably. She loved the water, a true Pisces, and we heard the first sweet sounds of enjoyment from her.

Bottle-feeding was easy. All the babies were hungry. Ali fell asleep at her last feeding and slept for eight hours . . . but we didn't. During the night we woke up several times to check on her breathing. Susie and I got up early and stood at the crib . . . looking at this amazing addition to our family . . . and waited. Finally, Ali woke up making happy, gentle, gurgling noises; not crying as most babies do. When she saw us looking at her in disbelief, she gave us a crooked smile. My heart had never been so full of love.

We had been told about bonding. For some children it can take days, weeks, months, and in rare cases, sadly . . . never. With Ali it was immediate. Susie and I felt an incredible love for this innocent child. She was a miracle.

After a short rest we were called to Ching's hotel room, where a Chinese notary was present. She asked many questions:

"Do you understand the undertaking of caring for this child? If you are working, how will the child be cared for? Do you want this baby?"

"YES! YES! YES!" came the unanimous answer from all of us.

I was the only Nai Nai, and enjoyed the title. It was miraculous that in only one day after being "grandchild-less" for almost seventy years, I was Nai Nai to five babies; even if only temporarily. In Ching's hotel room Susie thought she heard a remark that the orphanage had records and locations where each baby had been found. Susie immediately requested to visit the site where Ali had been left. In less than an hour Ching had a van and driver at our service to take us where each of the five infants had been abandoned, and found.

These innocent infants were forsaken at night with the hope that the mothers would not be caught in the illegal act of abandonment. If apprehended they would be punished and their entire families severely penalized, losing jobs and homes. It was 1996; China was a totalitarian communist country. The safest location for the babies to be found was outside police stations, hospitals, and schoolyards. Ali, at two weeks, was left in a box, lovingly wrapped in a blanket, in front of a food market. I cannot imagine a worse heart-wrenching situation then for a mother to give her baby up . . . never to gain knowledge of its whereabouts.

The owner of the store reported the discovery to the police as required by law. Ali was immediately taken to the orphanage. Ching read the report and cautioned us not to be too optimistic, as the proprietor might no longer be in business. We were lucky . . . he was.

Asian people are exceedingly polite. Business transactions take a long time. The first ten minutes of the talk is of niceties of the day, relatives, friends, until finally it is correct to get to the business at hand. For Westerners it can be frustrating . . . but we were warned of the custom.

Susie, holding Ali in her arms, and I beside her, watched Ching make conversation with Mr. Wong. He was a kind and gentle looking man, with big, round, dark eyes . . . probably in his thirties. It was obvious that when she got to the reason for our visit, Mr. Wong's focus went to the baby. Yes, he found the baby in a box in front of his business when he was about to open the store. Ching introduced us.

We shook hands all around. Mr. Wong seemed happy and animated that this child, that he had rescued, would live with us in the US. Suddenly I became aware that dozens of people had gathered around us, to hear the saga. Good news travels fast.

Again we heard, "Lucky baby. Lucky baby!" I smiled at the people and they politely bowed to us. With Mr. Wong's' permission I took photos of our hero, now a neighborhood celebrity, holding Ali in his arms. Susie promised that when Ali was older she would bring her to China with the hope of seeing him again. Public hugging and showing affection is unusual among Asians, but Mr. Wong did not resist our outpouring of love and respect toward him. He had a satisfied look on his pleasant face and waved to us as we left. We were lucky to have met him and will have photos to show Ali of her hero.

It had been a full and glorious day; one which changed our way of life irrevocably. Now when the five families met for dinner, the picture was different than even a day before. Having our meals became a bit complicated when holding a baby in our arms. We took turns holding the infants, some sleeping in their Snugglies, in order for the other adult to eat. Food suddenly became unimportant, but there were no complaints. We were thrilled with our new additions, and couldn't stop looking at our good fortune.

The following day we were busy going to several government offices. Since they were located nearby, we walked while holding our babies. The infants loved the closeness of the warm human body and the street air that put them to sleep. Susie and I took turns maneuvering. We heeded the good advice not to bring strollers. The cobblestone streets were narrow, wet, slippery, dirty and in ill repair. The pedestrians walked swiftly, bumped into each other, impolitely without apologies. The men in particular, had a bad habit of constantly spitting in the street. I found it unnerving and unsanitary. The street conditions while carrying the babies frightened me. My fear was of falling while carrying the babies. Luck was with us.

We stopped at the Immigration Health Clinic where all the babies were weighed, "examined" and pronounced healthy. The speed in which it was done was a farce. All of us were glad to get out of there. In the States we were all going to immediately see our pediatricians. Later the same day we walked to the Passport Office where the babies received their Chinese passports. In the US, with more paperwork, they would finally obtain a green card, and the much sought after US passport. We laughed about the green card.

At nine in the evening, several days later, we left Maoming for a nine-hour train trip back to the White Swan Hotel, in Guangzhou. We had to drag the luggage from the van through the parking lot into the train station, up the steps and onto the train . . . but this time we had additional precious cargo . . . the babies. It was difficult, but we all helped each other.

First class sleeper accommodations had been reserved for us. Each compartment had two double-decker-beds. Susie slept on top and I on the bottom. Ali was positioned against the wall, with lots of padding made from pillows and blankets. I snuggled up against her, and doubt that I slept much for fear of smothering my grandchild.

What fascinated me most on the train trip were the toilets. The Asian bathrooms had a hole in the floor, with a water hose and mop. It was crude and I decided to investigate the Western style. However, it was unbelievably filthy. Between the two, the Asian toilet won out.

There were several more offices to visit and more documents to sign. Throughout the process every Chinese official was helpful and kind. Finally we were ready for the US Consulate's office. All the previous offices were important, but this one made us nervous. This statesman had to approve of us, or we couldn't get the visa for the babies to leave China.

The moment our group walked into his office there were misunderstandings and friction. Everyone was American and of course spoke English. It should have been easy . . . but no. The secretary in a nasty tone complained that we were late. It was not so. We argued and she later apologized . . . she had made an error. But it was too late . . . the tone had already been set . . . the negative mood had been established.

The US Consulate was a racist, obnoxious man who made derogatory statements to every family he interviewed, always within earshot of all of us. It was obvious that he didn't like the Chinese, or his job. I had a feeling this was the last leg of his career and he couldn't wait for it to be over and retire. But we had to deal with his problem. He made fun of our paying $200 for visas, "for those babies," pointing at our precious Chinese infants, while our visas cost only $40. When he learned that Susie lived in Sarasota,

Florida, he said, "That used to be a nice state before they permitted busing." He referred to a couple with an obvious Jewish name as, ". . . you people."

We were all-livid, but kept quiet, out of fear. He could jeopardize our situation. Susie and I felt guilty for our silence. What could we do at that moment? We needed him to get Ali's visa.

Ten days after our arrival in Hong Kong we were ready to travel on our own, now that Ali had her visa. However there was one more hurdle to jump. Chinese citizens were not permitted to be in Hong Kong for more than five days. Airline reservations had to be made at the last minute. One never knew in advance how long they'd have to be in China to get all the paper work done . . . some people had stayed three weeks.

Ching was aware that we all wanted to get home as soon as possible. The first class seats for the train to Hong Kong were sold out, but that didn't deter her. She hired a touring bus and driver to take us to the Chinese New Territories border, which took less than three hours. At the border we left the bus . . . the driver stayed behind to protect our belongings. We walked to the Chinese Customs Declaration Building. Because of the babies' Chinese passports we had to go to a special line. Ching and Liza, who were Hong Kong citizens, had to go to another part of the building, not visible to us. Then the most grueling experience of the whole trip took place.

The five American families, with our Chinese babies, went to the proper line. I was the first and held all of Ali's papers. Susie had Ali in her soft baby carrier. The Chinese official understood no English. It was a new job . . . he had never seen these types of documents. He didn't know what to do with our records. Ching and Liza were in another building. We had no way to contact them. There we were on our own, with no knowledge of the procedure.

None of the officials were English speaking. The lines behind us were getting longer and longer. No supervisor was in sight. We stood still. People were getting annoyed with us . . . they couldn't move along . . . we were in their way. Finally the clerk took one batch of Ali's papers from me, and motioned our group to come through the line and wait at a designated area . . . *against the wall!* I was terrified, and kept my eyes on the papers.

Terrible thoughts went through my mind. The women clutching their babies, the men helpless, looked like refugees out of "Schindler's List," waiting to enter a cattle car . . . to a concentration camp. We were stuck. Nothing was happening. I didn't move. But I kept looking at Susie holding Ali . . . against that wall! The clerk had Ali's documents. My eyes were glued on him. Finally an official came and spoke to the clerk. He went to one of our men and demanded his baby's documents. Out of fear he wouldn't give them up. The official insisted on taking them . . . almost forced them out of Rob's hands. Rob, an impressive 6"4', strawberry blond man with deep blue eyes, had fire coming out of his mouth. He clutched the papers to his chest with both arms intertwined, raised his voice in a bellow, like King Kong, and screamed, "You can't have this! It's mine!"

I feared an incident. We all feared it. All of us understood Rob. The looks on our faces were pathetic. I didn't move from the side of the booth where the official was holding

Ali's papers. In my imagination I saw all of us in a Chinese jail.

The impasse was solved when the two officials finally communicated. A particular paper had been collected from each of us. One was missing. The official only wanted Rob's as a sample to show the first clerk. At last they realized that the missing paper was Ali's, the one I had my eye on. The clerk had had it all the time!

The final trauma occurred when the official looked at the tiny photo of the baby that appeared on the passport. He looked at each child intently; comparing the photo to the infant in front of him. He repeated that gesture again and again, and then made his evaluation. It was a match! Our nerves were frayed. Finally we walked over the border and out of China, to Hong Kong. It was exhausting, but we were gratefully able to breath freely again.

———

After eleven days we were on a flight to San Francisco. As we got to our seat, an attendant apologized to us profusely: an error had been made. We had reserved a bassinet for Ali, while still in the States, but the airline had botched the request.

"Would a cardboard box be okay?" the steward meekly asked.

"What?" we exclaimed incredulously.

This couldn't be happening. Ali practically came into the world in a box, and now she would arrive to the USA in a box again. What does this mean?

But beautiful wonderful things can come in boxes.

Since Ali was traveling on a Chinese passport we had to go through the immigration line. The American agent, with a broad smile on his face, looked at Ali's passport picture and then at Ali, and said, "Welcome to the United States, and Good luck."

FREEDOM!

Ali and I have something unique in common. I came to the United States because of religious persecution, and Ali because of the One-Child-Per Family law. Two different countries, for different reasons didn't want us. Ours was a true geographical relocation that gave us an opportunity for a new beginning.

We were both lucky.

Little Girl, Where Are You Going?

The streets of Manhattan are full of wonderment. Walking in the city is a joy . . . there is so much to see. If you don't concentrate, or are in a hurry to make the traffic light, you might miss an extraordinary experience. If you are a true New Yorker . . . you jaywalk when the opportunity presents itself.

Window-shopping is one of the greatest experiences in this great city. Some time ago, I walked on Madison Avenue . . . or was it Lexington? I noticed a new building that seemed to be all glass. The windows were huge and each one had a colorful abstract painting displayed facing the street. I observed a tiny, insignificant sign . . . Philip Morris Company (the tobacco company). Could this be?

My curiosity led me in. It was an exhibition of the most colorful abstracts I had ever seen. My usual reaction to art that pleases me is excitement. Did I feel my heart racing? I thought, *if only I could do that . . . can I?* To my surprise, these were not paintings but photographs, huge . . . four . . . five feet . . . or more. The glorious rich reds, sunny yellows, brilliant blues, and purples took my breath away.

165

Then I read the plaque . . . I couldn't believe it . . . this cannot be. The images were of *cancer cells* as seen under a microscope! How can something so evil, be so beautiful? My attitude toward these photographs changed. I became angry. How can nature be so cruel?

Red has always been my favorite color. But now, what am I to think? IS THIS ART? Is this what my Susie's cancer cells look like . . . beautiful, . . . as she is beautiful . . . like the ones I saw at the Philip Morris exhibition?

Sweet, curly haired little girl, where are you going? You're the child I always wanted. Since I was six-years-old, I had hopes of someday having a baby girl. I remember the time so well.

It was a Saturday, and I was visiting my mother's best friend, who had a fourteen-year-old daughter, Susie. That day she was nervous . . . she was getting dressed to go to her first dance party. For me, the six-year-old, it was a thrill to watch her put on a lovely sky-blue taffeta dress, which rustled when she moved, her first silk stockings and shoes with little heels. Her thick blond hair was bobbed, and a glittery barrette held it in place. She wore just a hint of pink lipstick. Oh, how I wanted to be in those shoes! I was envious. Inspired by that moment, I told myself; *if I ever have a girl, her name will be Susie.*

My first child was a boy. I was delighted with Jeffrey. He was a healthy, adorable, redheaded, exuberant child. When my jubilant parents came to the hospital to see their first grandchild, I shocked them by announcing, "*In three years I'm going to have a Susie.*"

I did. When my doctor happily informed me that he had just delivered my wish, I was overjoyed . . . I almost didn't believe him. How lucky I was. Now I had the perfect family: mother, father, a boy, and a girl.

Susie was the easiest, sweetest, brightest child to bring up. She had strawberry blond curly hair, rosy cheeks and intelligent, big, blue eyes. From the time she went to nursery school, I knew my little girl was going to be a teacher. Her dolls were her pupils. Writing and drawing on the big blackboard in her bedroom was her favorite activity. I knew then that she would be the perfect educator. And she was. One year, my Susie was voted the outstanding learning disability-teacher in her school district. She was completely devoted to those children, and wanted to adopt many of them.

But Susie took a longer route. In 1996, as a single woman, she adopted a baby girl from China. I accompanied her on that trip. Up to that time, it was the most profound decision Susie ever made. She named the child Ali, after my husband, Al. She's been an adorable, intelligent, and well-behaved child . . . now she's a fourteen-year-old teenager. The relationship between mother and daughter is beautiful.

Suddenly everything changed.

What has happened to my precious curly haired child? Why is she leaving us? Where is she going . . . and so soon? Every day we lose some of Susie. Her hair falls out in clumps. In the past three months her body has played horrible tricks. Medications and treatments are constantly changed . . . to no avail. With little energy remaining, she does whatever she can to make life pleasant. My child doesn't deserve the pain she is enduring. Susie has always been a good and thoughtful person. Now her eyes and thoughts are on Ali. Our family and friends, who love her dearly, cringe at the thought that this child, abandoned at birth for political reasons, will again be without a mother . . . twice in fourteen years.

After a valiant four-month struggle, Susie died in 2010. She was fifty-four-years-old.

No Coffin . . . Please

I refused to go to the cemetery, but my mother forced me. After my eighty-six-year-old grandmother died, my mother wished to visit her grave, and for me to accompany her. I was sixteen, and preferred to spend time with my friends. She insisted that I to go with her.

"I want to stay home."

"You can't. You have to come with me."

"I don't want to."

"That's very disrespectful . . . it's your grandmother."

"My not going doesn't show disrespect. I can remember her here in my room and think about her."

"You are ungrateful."

I didn't want to remember Oma at all. She was a nasty, unloving woman, not the kind, cuddly grandmothers my girlfriends had. The last five years of her life I had to share my bedroom with her. When she moved into my sanctuary, she placed her false teeth in a glass jar on top of my dresser, and her ugly "sheitel," (wig that Orthodox Jewish married women wear) that she aired out on a wooden block . . . every night. I hated it. My mother wants me to "visit" her.

No, thanks. Now that I have my room back, I want to stay there, and enjoy my freedom.

This is how my mother and I communicated. She made demands and left no wiggle room for me to change her mind. Of course, I ended up going with her. What choice did I have?

At that young age I made a decision: I will be cremated. My children will never feel the guilt about not going to "visit" me at the cemetery.

Many decades have passed since I was a teenager. When my children became adults we talked about our end-of-life wishes. My "Living Will" spelled out everything. I wanted to be cremated. Jeffrey and Susie expressed the same. It felt good that I took care of everything, no surprises, all questions already answered. My children will not have to guess, "What did Mom want . . . what did she mean by that . . ." All was clear. Considering our ages, I would go first.

Sometimes life plays tricks. The unthinkable happened. Susie at fifty-four, was the first to go. She left us. How could this happen? Two weeks before she died, when she was still lucid, I had the opportunity to ask her questions.

"Susie, do you remember what I requested when I die?"

"Of course, Mom, I remember. You want to be cremated." She shook her head of strawberry curls in agreement. At that moment she looked like a mature Shirley Temple.

"Yes, that's so."

"And you want a memorial party with food . . . lots of garlic." We laughed but were not surprised at my request. Good food has always been important in our family.

"You do remember." I was impressed since my children aren't great in the memory department. We tease each other about that.

"You asked for music . . . Beethoven, Mozart, Gershwin, and Leonard Bernstein . . . all at Jeffrey's house."

"Exactly . . . and what do you want?"

"As I mentioned in my Living Will, I want cremation, and a happy memorial party."

"Do you want the Celebration of Life to be at Jeffrey's house?"

"Oh, no! His house and garden are too small. I want it at Laurel Park, with live music and pot-luck food," That surprised me.

And so it was, with more than 200 people attending.

———

Cremation is not a Jewish ritual, except for the reformed, or atheists. Our family all agreed. We still have not decided what to do with her remains. I have a feeling that we are waiting until after the first anniversary of her death.

Although I designated in my Living Will that I wanted cremation, the thought sometimes feels creepy. *My body burning and going up in smoke . . . is that what I really want? But then the alternative . . . being buried in a casket forever . . . my body slowly deteriorating . . . the bugs having good meals . . . the decay . . . is that better?* Mulling it over, cremation seemed the better option.

I suddenly remembered an incident forty years ago. When my husband and I passed a vast cemetery in an exclusive part of Brooklyn, I exclaimed, "Look, that's a waste of good real estate." He agreed.

~~~~~~~~

Jeffrey has visited India and Nepal and has seen cremations at the river's edge; an everyday occurrence in those countries. I never asked him what his reaction was. Now I'm trying to visualize the procedure.

Suddenly I think of Susie's beautiful strawberry curls. In 1958, when she was three, she wanted "a big girl, Pixie" short haircut . . . no more ponytail. I took 8 mm movies of the occasion. Today I remembered where the ponytail is . . . I saved it . . . in my jewelry box . . . all these years.

The more I think, the more I remember. Years ago Susie asked to borrow a ring from me. As we went through my jewelry box I came across the ponytail. She was surprised that I had saved it.

It's bizarre . . . although she is cremated, a physical part of Susie is with me right now . . . her beautiful strawberry blond curly pony tail.

They can't take that away from me.

THE WEDDING DRESS

September 17, 2010

W hy am I torturing myself? What is the point? With the flick of my finger, I can erase the agony, but I stay with it for an hour. I will bring this up at my next session with the grief counselor. The visits have been helpful . . . I can speak about anything that is bothering me . . . without concern about how the person I'm discussing might feel. At this time I need that freedom.

I was clicking TV channels and stopped at, "Say YES to the Dress." It's a reality show: brides at a salon that has an inventory of over 1,500 gowns come with their entourages to choose their wedding dress. As a former dress designer, I found the client's tastes fascinating, surprising, and sometimes atrocious. With my interest in psychology and storytelling, I saw the frustrations between mothers and daughter (sometimes fathers), siblings, best friends, and future mothers-in-law. Some brides came with a group of ten. Being naïve, they didn't realize that it made it more difficult to make a decision, with more opinions . . . more frustrations . . . more baffling . . . more insecurity.

When I was getting married, I went shopping with only my mother, which was one more person than I generally shopped with. So typically a New York shtick, she took me to a showroom of a "friend's friend," who owned an exclusive evening gown manufacturing company, where she was able to get my dress at the wholesale price. Luckily we both liked the same gown. I shudder to think what would have happened if that had not been the case.

On the television show, two brides broke down because they had recently lost their mothers; missed them terribly, especially at such an important time in their lives, and couldn't on their own decide which dress to buy?

As they did, I too cried. Watching this episode broke my heart. It pushed my vulnerable button. I was thinking of my Susie. We never brought up the subject of marriage. I never asked. My friends and relatives couldn't understand my attitude; as if I didn't care. I did care, but it was not my business. And I didn't want to interfere in their lives, (Jeffrey's, as well). I felt it was respectful to keep quiet. Sooner or later they would give me the wonderful news.

I think if Susie ever thought about getting married, she wouldn't have wanted a traditional wedding gown . . . more likely a vintage dress . . . perhaps from a consignment shop? It's doubtful if she would have asked for my opinion . . . but in this case . . . maybe. Twenty-four years ago when Jeffrey was getting married, Susie and I went shopping for a dress for her to wear to her brother's wedding. We agreed that nothing we saw impressed us in the six stores we visited. The clock was ticking . . . the date was quickly approaching, but I knew we'd find the dress . . . and we did . . . unexpectedly at an Art Fair. In total agreement Susie and I said, "Yes to the Dress."

Susie was independent. I usually found out about the most important decisions in her life: buying houses, traveling alone to exotic places in South America and Vietnam, adopting a baby from China, and inviting Karim to move in with her . . . after the fact. However, I would have approved of a vintage dress, and all the above. I knew her, and yet . . . sometimes . . . not. How can I complain . . . she got that independent gene from me?

Unfortunately . . . it never happened. *Oh, Susie, how beautiful you would have looked, no matter what you wore . . . with your strawberry curls and unbelievable smile . . . maybe as big as the smile you had when you held Ali in your arms after we landed at the Sarasota Airport, coming home from China . . . and you showing her off . . . like the best prize anyone ever received.* Without saying it, her demeanor conveyed: *Look at this beautiful baby that I brought back from Asia!* Her many friends would have been thrilled to come to the wedding, (as they did to the airport in 1996, for Ali's debut) with amazingly great vegetarian food, exciting live music, and lots of love.

I think Ali would have been happy for her mother to be married. She wanted her family to be what she considered a *real family*. When Ali was two, she asked Susie for a daddy. As she got older, she felt it easier to refer to Karim as her dad when she introduced him. A few years ago Ali told me that after she graduated from college, and had a good job, she'd want to get married, and *then* have children.

And so I cried then, and cry now. It hurts so much to think of those glorious events . . . that never happened . . . and never will. The sequence in our lives was incorrect. I should have been the first to go. One should never experience the death of a child. Susie brought that home when she related her gruesome medical news to me . . . "Mom, I'm dying. You shouldn't have to go through this ordeal with me." I cradled her into my arms, thinking of the first time I saw her, fifty-four years ago . . . *I'm so lucky to have the baby girl I always wanted.* I cried from happiness then, and now . . . *How can this be happening?*

It all went so unbelievably fast . . . she was gone within four months. FOUR MONTHS! We were hoping for at least several years. It's two years since she left us. I still expect Susie to come to my door. She has the key.

BITS
AND
PIECES

Whͮᴀᴛ Dᴏ Yᴏᴜ Tʜɪɴᴋ?

Oh, no! . . . Please, don't come in NOW . . . it's five minutes before closing. But they don't feel my negative vibes, and enter. I can't say anything . . . it's against store policy . . . I'll probably have to change my plans for tonight.

You should see what they look like . . . certainly not like our usual customer, in this most exclusive, one-of-a-kind, art-to-wear boutique. I love working here, being surrounded by beautiful clothing made by artists. If appearance is indicative, these two people are in the wrong store.

He's probably in his forties, short, an ordinary face with the European sexy 5 o' clock shadow, unkempt thick dark hair, and his physique wouldn't take anyone's breath away. The tennis shirt needs to go into the laundry . . . together with the dirty white shorts and white socks. The scruffy brown shoes should walk themselves to the cobbler. Goodwill should be his destination.

His *zaftig* female companion, in her twenties, has a pleasant cherubic face that shows off her sparkling dark eyes and a shock of curly, shoulder-length brown hair.

This dumpling is short, a good height for him, with lots of energy and an engaging smile. Looking at them . . . it's easy to see what he sees in her. They're well matched. She's wearing a summer print dress with spaghetti straps. I notice a safety pin at one shoulder. This is not for artistic effect . . . she's a slob. Actually she's wearing two dresses, layered on top of each other, the hems uneven and torn, showing off her chubby thighs. She needs a pedicure. Visually I am turned off by their appearance but somehow I'm enchanted with them. I like the way they look at each other. Their attraction feels genuine. I assume this is a new romance . . . a relationship in progress . . . wanting to please each other. He's showing his power by leading her, and she's acquiescing to his whims . . . a well-matched disheveled pair. But what are they doing in this exclusive establishment?

First stop . . . he leads her to the sale rack. *Watch out young lady with the big brown eyes. He's cheap. Hear me, I know . . . you can't change that . . . it's in his DNA. Nothing good will come of it . . . no matter how charming or sexy he might be . . . I know.*

He's the scout, looking through the racks and picking out items for his companion to try on. With her beautiful, large, dark gypsy eyes, she looks at me and whispers, "I have no taste in clothes. I'll try on anything he wants me to." I give her extra points for being honest. Or is she playing the dumb beauty?

I get a fitting room ready. He follows me with several garments over his arm. She's anxious to try them on. When she comes out of the room I see the garment is too tight on her. I'm about to say, "I'll get the next size" . . . but he loves the way she looks . . . stuffed into the clothes that show off her voluptuous curves. (Suddenly I remember being eight years old, watching my mother in the kitchen . . . stuffing . . . forcing . . . chopped meat into the goose's neck . . . to be baked and served for the holiday.) She hops into the dressing room to try on the next selection. I love her exuberance. My associate and I watch. This is more fun than my date this evening would have been.

He pulls me aside and confides, "She has a great job . . . she's a lawyer, but has terrible taste in clothes. Help me find some things she can wear to the office." *She's a lawyer? And goes out of the house looking like this?* The show takes on more meaning.

It's closing time, my associate locks the front entrance and flips the door sign from OPEN to CLOSED. My clients realize that they have the whole place to themselves. She loves it. Now she is free to try on each garment that her lover hands her and parades around the store . . . preening from one mirror to another. No longer does she bother to change in the fitting room. She kicks off her shoes, prances around in her bare feet, wearing only a bra and panties. Her eyes glow with excitement. I'm getting the hang of what he wants her to look like. I bring him armloads of garments. My tactics work.

Every time he likes something on her, he hands it to me and says, "We'll take it." I put the yes's on the counter. The pile is getting high. One would think the garments are bargains. He decides not to take anything from the sale rack. *I was wrong about him being cheap. It was obvious from the beginning that he was going to pay. Could he have been testing her?*

181

My adrenalin is soaring. I'm trying to figure out how much money the committed items will add up to. Each time he says, "We'll take this," she hugs him. She's getting more and more amorous, and he's getting a bit embarrassed in front of us. If he continues to purchase more clothes, and she continuous to grab him so ardently, we might see the unexpected, right in front of us. There is a video monitor. What a story this will make for tomorrow!

Our policy is to continue to "feed" customers merchandise until they say, "That's it . . . No more." The time has come. I go to the computer to ring up the sale when suddenly the paramour slips on a red fur jacket . . . over her printed, summer dress. What a look . . . I can't believe it! Her face shows it all . . . she looks adorable . . . cuddly . . . innocent. She's "Lolita" . . . *do what you wish with me!* She hops over to her lover, takes his hand and puts it on the fur to stroke it. "Isn't it de.li.ci.ous?" she coos, looking into his eyes. He can't resist her, and takes the fur gently off her body and adds it to the growing mountain of clothes on the counter. She's ecstatic, jumps on him, wraps her arms around his neck and lets her legs dangle off the floor . . . like a rag doll. The look on his face reads, *I'm making her happy . . . It's only money.*

"Do you want this sent, or do you wish to take it with you?" I ask him.

Before the question is answered, she grabs the red fur from the counter and puts it on over her awful dress. She wraps herself in it like a bathrobe. Innocently she asks me, "Can I wear it out of the store?"

Florida is hot in September, but she's a little girl wanting to lick her lollypop right now.

"Of course you can." I feel righteous and tell her, "It's paid for."

She's jumping up and down like a six-year-old. He looks at the credit card statement and immediately signs it. They choose to take everything with them. All the goodies are on hangers, and then placed into several garment bags.

We all hug and kiss. Everyone is happy. My associate unlocks the front door to let the clients out ninety minutes after closing. He goes first, holding all the bags. She follows.

Suddenly she stops and takes me aside. Confidentially she says, "We've only known each other six months. What do you think . . . is he going to dump me?"

"No way," I say. "He just invested twelve thousand dollars. You're safe."

For a while at least!

THE GLORIOUS FISH

She was used to last minute phone calls and actually enjoyed them. It reassured her that this job was going well. That was her boss, the firm's sales manager, on the line. He needed her again after work, to meet him at his favorite watering hole. A very important buyer was joining him there. She was essential as his designer to listen to their conversations pertaining to new styles the client might want.

He was a great boss in spite of the fact that he was an alcoholic, as was this merchant. Although only in his twenties, the buyer was smart and already had a position with the largest, most prestigious catalogue house in the country. The future looked good for him (*if he controlled his drinking*). Getting one order from him easily paid the annual salaries for the boss and the designer.

The dress designer was fortunate that her employer knew how to deal with his addiction . . . never drank before noon . . . was aware that there would be much conversation, and didn't want to rely on his memory the next morning.

Besides being creative, his designer had to be all ears. It was not an easy task, but exciting and gratifying.

It was also her good fortune that her husband understood the situation and didn't object to getting last minute calls canceling dinner. He was proud of his wife, and her flourishing career.

Her boss was already at the popular Italian restaurant frequented by top executives as well as the Mafia of the New York garment industry. At any time of the day or night, the restaurant was a safe place because of the underworld connection, and as a bonus . . . it had a great bar.

By the time the designer entered the brasserie, the two men had already had a few. That was not obvious by their demeanor, but rather by their habit of lining up the empty glasses in front of them at the bar. It was a childish game they played, probably to keep track of their consumption. As soon as the designer came through the door and before she even sat down, the two men made room for her between them. Although she was sophisticated, always dressed like out of the pages of *Vogue*, she had never mastered how to get on and off a barstool gracefully; and felt like a klotz.

A Black Russian was already waiting for her. The bartender knew she would nurse the one drink all evening. He didn't object, knowing that her boss was a big tipper and lunched there almost daily (often all liquid). At this watering hole, there were no secrets. Everyone knew everyone's "business," but details were kept under cover, whether legal or illicit.

An hour and many Dewars later, the boss gallantly threw several big bills on the bar, hailed a cab for the three of them, and informed the driver to take them to The Palm, the most outlandishly expensive, popular steak/ seafood restaurant in town. No matter how many drinks the boss had consumed, he always acknowledged that his designer had to eat. The buyer, however, didn't care where they went, as long as his glass was constantly refilled. The cost of the evening did not matter as long as her sales manager "nailed" the account. The business allowed him a generous expense account. There was important work to discuss.

Although her boss loved lobster or a twenty-eight ounce steak that always overlapped the extra size dinner plate, he loved his Dewars more. He also knew that his designer loved fish. Not just any good filet of sole, but a whole fish, head to tail, with all the bones intact. This restaurant was one of the few in the city that was equipped to grant such a request.

They were happily greeted by the maître d' who seated them at one of the best tables, shoehorned together with other tables, in order to be elbowed by "important" people in the industry. In this bistro, the closer, the better . . . the better to hear what the competition had to say. Of course everyone spoke in telephone numbers. Everything in this place was exaggerated. It had the atmosphere of a cocktail party, but you sat, and the food was sublime. The men ordered more drinks, as well as another Black Russian (which she never consumed), while the designer waited for her whole trout, prepared just as requested. She noted that the waiter was skeptical and asked if she *really* wanted the head and tail on, and not filleted? "Yes, of course . . . head . . . tail . . . bones . . . all of it . . . intact . . . absolutely!" she said with a broad smile. With that affirmative statement, did she see him wink at her as he took the order?

When she was a young girl, her father taught her how to eat a whole fish without choking on the bones. He was a good teacher and she, an observant, attentive pupil. Large pieces of rye bread were always on the table in case a bone got lodged in some one's the throat. In that painful, frightful, situation, forcibly swallowing a chunk of chalah or rye bread, followed immediately with some cold seltzer (dispensed from the ubiquitous siphon bottle) did the trick.

She was completely absorbed in doing surgery on the trout. The fish was so large that its head and tail hung over the large plate, almost touching the starched white tablecloth. Methodically she took the skin off, cut it into bite size portions, slowly lifted her fork, and looked at the delicacy before each bite came to her mouth. She ate it leisurely and frequently licked her lips. Like an engineer, she had a definite plan in mind. Of course she remembered her father's lesson and slowly scooped up the luscious meat, working the fork from under the head to the tail. The fish maven scrutinized each portion before bringing it to her mouth and continued to eat without hurry, or concern about time. Her eyes never left her plate, but she heard the men's conversation. However, at one point they weren't talking business anymore; actually they had stopped speaking. They watched in amazement as she performed surgery.

When she finished eating the first half, the fish was turned over on its other side, and the remainder was dissected. Then came the best part . . . like dessert. First she picked up the tail, which had some meat on it, brought it to her mouth and played it like a harmonica, back and forth, until it was dry. The designer enjoyed every morsel. Next came the head, which had such sweetness between the eyes that most people don't know, or care to know about. Carefully she extracted the eyes and placed them gently to the side of the plate. For a moment she thought of taking the eyes home and using them in a collage she was working on. They were so clear because the fish was fresh. Using good judgment, she decided not to eat them . . . after all . . . she wasn't home. Chinese consider it a delicacy, but most American found the act gross.

At this point, all that was left was the carcass. The artist in her looked at her plate and saw a beautiful Matisse still life. She took a deep breath and broke it into pieces, picked it up, and inch, by inch, moaned softly, sucked at it and licked it with her tongue, flicking back and forth until it was barren. Gently she put the bones back on her plate in a straight line. That reminded her of a Picasso she saw at MoMA on a recent visit. Her eyes were shining with delight as she licked her lips, gently wiped her mouth and gracefully placed the napkin on the table. She was finished.

Unhurried she looked up and saw both men, as well as the people at the next table, looking at her. A little smirk appeared on her face as she met their eyes. How long had they been watching her?

Her boss broke the silence. "I wish I was that fish."

Master Class

The old geezer sits in front of me in the concert hall. I'm in the second row, left of center, in order to see the fingering of the pianist. We're waiting. I notice the man's brassy, red-orange unruly dyed hair. While waiting he turns his head, scans the hall, as if he's searching for someone. I take a closer look . . . he fascinates me . . . he must be over ninety. His hair is long and curly on the sides but his dome has strands that stick up in a Mohawk. I wonder how he sees himself when looking in the mirror . . . or does he?

His attention shifts front and center as a twenty-something student comes out of the wings, slowly walks on stage, making her way to the grand piano. I'm annoyed; she fidgets with the knob of the stool . . . up and down . . . it seems like forever. Finally she sits down. She closes her eyes, takes a deep breath and places her long fingers on the keyboard. I envy her tapered hands; mine are short, almost childlike. The master class begins. As soon as she starts to play Mozart's Concerto in C Minor, I know I'm in the presence of an extraordinary artist.

191

The geezer is bewitched too. Is he beguiled because she plays with passion, or is his passion aroused because he notices the long slit on her navy skirt that exposes her slender right leg? The young performer is no fashion plate, wearing a shabby green wrinkled shirt over a brown polo. The dull blond hair is pulled back haphazardly with enumerable black bobby pins. Her head looks like an art-nouveau piece of sculpture. At nine in the morning her heavily applied makeup is out of place at a master class. She looks like a "woman of the evening" after a long night. The old man is moving his head to the rhythm of the music as I enjoy the breathtaking performance. When the piece ends I feel fortunate to have experienced this outstanding recital. The handful of people in the audience applauds enthusiastically.

All is quiet now. Again we wait. During this time of the performance the maestro sat in the concert hall, listening, watching . . . showing no reaction.

The silence is broken by a thump of the maestro clumsily jumping onto the stage. He's no athlete, flat-footed, but has enormous energy and enthusiasm. The professor is in his forties. He, too, is a sight. Although in Florida, his face has prison pallor, like a Talmudic student who's never been kissed by the sun. A pince-nez over his beady eyes would be comfortable on his narrow pinched nose, and the sand colored hair, parted in the center, reminds me of Alfalfa of "The Little Rascals." The face is almost hairless but not feminine; thin arms gyrate out of his tee shirt, short khaki green cargo pants expose his knobby knees, beige short socks and the perennial black patent leather shoes amuse me. I can easily visualize the maestro as a twelve-year old Cub Scout.

Suddenly he raises his thin arms enthusiastically; his longish hair flies as he does an impromptu dance. He's no Baryshnikov. I listen and watch. The maestro explains the musical selection to the student while constantly moving about the stage, back and forth, like an expectant father. I know his impressive credentials: Professor of Humanities at Harvard University, faculty member at the Curtis Institute and SUNY, Purchase, historian, linguist, concert pianist, lecturer, and more. At fourteen he was invited by Nadia Boulanger to move to Europe and became her student. He remained for ten years.

The pupil plays the piece by heart. And we find out in a moment that the maestro, without the musical score, knows every note and marking.

He scoots to the piano, his arms dangling, his head leaning forward, like a turtle . . . makes eye contact with his pupil to vacate the piano bench . . . sits and plays selections that he feels can be improved. At times he terrorizes the piano, cajoles the keys, makes the instrument sing or cry, and when needed, strokes it gently like a sensitive lover. It is sheer magic. He's aware that we are a receptive audience . . . he plays right into it.

The maestro's knowledge of composers, the history of their lives and personal stories is astonishing. The information is not planned; it spurts out whenever the occasion is suitable. To add to his impressive attributes, he has an uncanny sense of humor.

I suddenly remember at one of his lectures some time ago he surprised everyone by casually stating he has only a bachelor's degree, and referred to himself as, "a *schmendrek* from Brooklyn." This *schmendrek* has recorded the entire Mozart repertoire!

At times he preaches, "Learn your music slowly . . . start with the expression . . . be patient with yourself . . . feelings come first . . . notes follow." When a selection wasn't played to his liking, he commented: "Walk first . . . run afterwards." Emphasizing the score, he mentions color, space and taste. He suggests: visit museums, look at paintings and notice their rhythm and color.

"Don't make a mistake between applesauce and celery," he quips. The student looks confused, and he explains, "Don't get more interested in your left hand when your right hand is playing." The young music student understands the advice, replays the passage, and the instant change is awesome. I'm mesmerized.

My attention was totally with what was happening on stage. Then I realize that I forgot all about the old geezer in front of me. I look. He's still there. At the conclusion of the master class I'm glued to my seat . . . I'm not ready to break the spell and get up. But the spell is broken when the maestro suddenly jumps off the stage and lands right in front of the old geezer. To my surprise they hug warmly. I hear part of their affectionate conversation, and come to the conclusion: "Once upon a time . . . many years ago" . . . the geezer had been the maestro's teacher.

Iced Coffee

I don't understand. What's so difficult about getting a good, strong, glass of iced coffee? You'd be surprised. In New York City it's a standard request, but I learned not to take such things for granted. My favorite drink, summer and winter, is a tall glass of strong, iced, decaffeinated coffee, with a bit of half & half, and lots of ice. You think that's easy? Well, let me tell you, if you think that . . . you're wrong.

Forty years ago, I traveled to South America. It was December, winter in New York, summer in Chile. Latinos drink lots of soda, especially Coca-Cola, hot coffee, and mixed alcoholic drinks. Ice cream and ices are also favorites.

Sitting at the counter, feeling very American, I thought this would be the perfect place to get my drink of choice. Wrong! With my high school Spanish I asked for *café frio*. Little did I know that *frio* means cold . . . temperature, as in weather. They gave me ice cream. "No. No." Then I asked for a glass with *hielo* (ice) and a cup of hot coffee *con leche*. Their startled faces told me that they didn't believe me. I repeated my request, and reluctantly the bartender gave me the items. With a bit of drama, I placed an ice cream spoon into the glass containing the ice cubes, and carefully poured the hot coffee over it to prevent the glass from cracking.

Several people surrounded me as if I were a magician or from outer space. I was called *una gringa loca.* I understood the expression and laughed. Now I had an audience. They watched me drink my concoction with disbelief. When I guzzled it down and had an expression of delight on my face, the people clapped. I bowed. It was an unexpected fun performance.

Four years ago, I returned to Chile. After four decades, I thought that surely my request would be easily understood. Wrong. At a museum coffee shop, after a native Chilean explained to the waiter what I wanted, I received an exquisite presentation of an ice cream soda in a beautiful tall crystal glass, with whipped cream, shaved chocolate and an edible flower as garnish. It was delicious, but it was not what I had in mind. Not to embarrass any one, I consumed it . . . slowly . . . savoring every spoonful . . . with guilt. Those sumptuous calories were fabulous.

On another occasion on this trip, my Chilean friend very explicitly explained to her maid what I wanted. I received a glass of soda water and hot coffee. In South America, one must specify when you order bottled water, whether you want *con,* or *sin gas.* Several times at a restaurant, I was given carbonated water when all I wanted was ice cubes. When I realized how complicated my wish for iced coffee was, I never asked for it to be decaffeinated. Can you imagine the confusion that that would have presented?

Only once during the ten-day trip did I get what I asked for. It amazed me. I congratulated the waiter, who then told me that he had lived in California for several years. My trip to Chile was outstanding; however, it was great to get back to the States and have my beloved iced coffee.

Gringa loca.

THERE'S NO FREE LUNCH

Look at her! Do you see what I see? I can't take my eyes off her . . . I'm compelled to stare . . . and at him as well. They are an unlikely looking couple. The Woman's arm entwines his. Maybe they're European. I like cosmopolitan nonchalance . . . sophisticated . . . and it looks like fun.

She sashays into the fashion boutique and makes a beeline for the first sales associate. It's a calculating move but she's graceful. Maybe she was a dancer. I guess The Woman to be in her fifties . . . six-feet . . . statuesque . . . an Anita Ekberg look-a-like . . . well kept . . . in more ways than one. Scandinavian . . . the three B's: blond . . . blue eyed . . . bosomy. Her large, puffy Cupid collaged lips fascinate me. Her mouth looks like an exotic fish sucking on the glass of an aquarium.

Before The Man disengages his arm from hers, I notice that his bald head reaches her bosom . . . a comforting place for him to be. He sits down on the deep upholstered chair, placed strategically for this purpose. The shop owner understands the psychology of her customers. He has experience. In front of The Man is a cocktail table with the latest fashion magazines, the local paper, *New York Times,* and *The Wall Street Journal.* His face is long and narrow, and his eyes become slits when he smiles. The nose is small, the lips, thin. He does have something big . . . gigantic . . . elephant ears! The Couple look like cartoon characters. I guess him to be in his seventies, well preserved. His muscle shirt shows off his broad shoulders and abs. The well-cut tight jeans make him look virile, and taller than he is. The Man takes care of himself. I admire him . . . he's not with a twenty-year-old trophy wife.

I look at The Woman and notice a lack of character in her face . . . *how many face lifts has she had?* At least she has some muscle control and is able to move her lips . . . even can give us a little smile. Her white-blond hair accentuates the blunt cut bangs across her smooth Botox forehead that just skims the tattooed dark eyebrows and eyeliner. In case of fire, she's made up for any occasion. The hair, just a fraction above her shoulder, is horizontally blunt-razor-cut. Perfect.

As my eyes travel down her body, I notice her beautifully designed blue cashmere scoop-neck sweater, which coordinates with her blue contact lenses. Of course they're contacts . . . no one's eyes are such a vivid blue. Her outfit is not too tight, nor the neck too low. Her matching long skirt has thigh high slits skimming her narrow hips to expose her beautifully shaped long legs, and of course she is wearing seven-inch stiletto sandals. How does she maneuver in those shoes? It's a trick that I've never been able to master. She stands above us all. I'm mesmerized by fashion, but I've never been this fascinated by a woman. The Woman's outstanding.

"Helloooo! It's so gooood to see you again," sings out the first saleswoman she approaches.

"Hello, to you, too!" she answers with enthusiasm.

"We haven't seen you for a time," says another.

"Right. We haven't been in town for a while. My Lovey bought a magnificent three-bedroom apartment for us . . . on one of those luxury liners . . . *The World.* You've seen them . . . in the travel magazines. *The New York Times* had a three-page article about the grand ship that continuously cruises around the world. If we wish, we could stay on her forever," she reports proudly.

"That sounds magnificent," the manager agrees. On hearing the conversation from her office, she quickly joins all of us. She feels the vibes . . . the sweet smell of $$$!

"Yes, it's unbelievable. We have the boat's schedule. No . . . no . . . I shouldn't call it a boat . . . it's a gigantic ship . . . the largest floating vessel in the world . . . with a crew of a thousand . . . for only four hundred passengers."

"My goodness! . . . That's great," one of the customers chimes in. There's a whole group of women sizing her up.

"Yes. We look at the port-of-call list when we wish to travel. Then we fly to the destination of our choice . . . and board the ship. Depending on the location, sometimes we're picked up by helicopter. Usually we have an almost empty copter or a small plane, because I have so many pieces of luggage. I really don't need to pack much because I leave closets full of clothing on the ship of our apartment. But of course I always need some new things . . . you ladies understand that. Everything has to be weight, including us when we travel by helicopter or small planes . . . Isn't that a scream? I fast the day before we travel.

In some locations it is futile for us to use our large jet because the airstrips in these remote destinations are so small. Of course I don't have to concern myself about those facts . . . my Lovey has people who take care of everything. But it's interesting."

"It certainly is. Tell us more."

"I always get friendly with the pilot and tell him not to do any tricks in the air. I once had a scary experience . . . don't' even want to remember it."

"Oh?"

"Anyway . . . everything's great. Our apartment at sea can accommodate many friends. Just imagine, being at the most luxurious Ritz Carlton . . . floating in the middle of the ocean."

"Hm . . . sounds like a dream." *What does something like that cost?*

"Is it a time-share?" asks a client.

"Oh no! You buy it. It's like a condo. You own it completely . . . use it when it's convenient. I've invited many of my girlfriends . . . now that's better than 'A night out with the girls.' They can stay as long as I'm on board. Usually I do that when my Lovey doesn't have time to join me . . . but I do."

"Really . . . A condo that floats?"

"Yes. My Lovey and I just came back from a three months cruise." She beckons us to get closer to her, and lowers her voice. *Is she about to tell us a secret?* "To tell the truth . . . it can get *really* boring out there . . . days without seeing land. That's another reason to invite friends." *Put me on that list!*

The sound of Sousa's music brings me back to reality. It's coming from The Man's cell phone. He answers it immediately.

"You bet, Tyler. We'll just charge him fifty percent more. Yes, Yes. He'll spring . . . sure . . . sure . . . you bet. Yep . . . we'll get it. You're right . . . the guys locked into the deal . . . no other place for him to go . . . I agree . . . He needs us. So long." The Man has a sly smirk on his face as he hangs up.

The Woman is having a ball. She's obviously used to being the center of attention. I bet she's a former Las Vegas Showgirl. Look how she's put together, and how she prances like a Kentucky Derby winner. On her left hand she sports a simple gold wedding band. That surprises me. I'd expect a *serious* bauble. She's so very friendly. We watch her each time she comes out of the fitting room, sporting a new magnificent outfit. Our "ohs" and "ahs" make her smile. With her body . . . everything looks great.

At close glance, I see her other hand. Now there . . . there's an embellishment one can get blinded by . . . The Knocker! . . . The largest, most sparkling diamond I've ever seen. It covers half her finger. A yenta would ask, "Is

it for real . . . how much did he shell out for that bauble? "
I must admit . . . I'd like to know.

"What do you mean he's going on vacation?" The Man
raises his voice. He's on the phone again. "I know . . . I
know . . . He's mothballed us twice before. This deal is
more important than *shtupping* his bulimic girlfriend. Did
you ever see that dame? You haven't? . . . well . . . she has
implants that look like watermelons . . . she can't even stand
up straight. Tell him to cut the crap . . . No contract . . . no
damn vacation . . . no job."

With fury he snaps the cell cover down. It pops into his
face and drops to the floor. In an instant The Man leaps
off the chair and retrieves it. He puts it right back . . . he's
fast . . . just like his temper. His raucous outburst gets my
attention. He has nice buns. The cushioned chair is too deep
for him . . . his legs dangle. I notice his alligator shoes . . .
no socks. He must have been a funny looking kid. Now
he's still funny looking, but he can buy the World.

In the meantime, The Woman announces in a wispy,
girly voice, that her husband asked her what she wanted
for her birthday. "I said, 'Lovey, fly me in our jet to my
favorite shop and let me loose.' And here I am. He allowed
me two hours to do as much damage as I wish. My Lovey
doesn't want me to ask his opinion on the clothes. He said,

'Don't bother me . . . ask the ladies if you need help . . . I'm busy.' Isn't that sweet?" she gushes.

The Man's cell phone is doing the marching thing again. My focus is on The Woman. She tells her awe-struck-audience her needs: special occasion outfits for several galas, two weddings and numerous private parties. Activities accelerate in and out of the fitting room. She pirouettes in front of the three-way mirror for her attentive audience. Time is fleeting and there's so much more to buy.

The Woman has a great figure. She would look elegant in burlap. The saleswomen "feed" clothes to her . . . like a conveyor belt. Wine is served, and with it . . . in short order . . . comes loud laughter. Everyone's getting loose. The star performer is quickly on her third drink and giggles like a mischievous spoiled little girl. She's fun.

"We married nine months ago; I for the third time, and my Lovey for the fifth. But I know for sure . . . this one's going to stick." *Sure honey.* "We're still on our honeymoon," she shyly brags and winks her baby-blues. *Who wants to bet?*

The Man doesn't drink. Both the sales help and the customers are focused on The Woman's purchasing adventure. The "ohs" and "ahs" continue and drown out the store's music. She tries on another magnificent outfit, never looking at the price tag. *Oh, to have her priceless figure. Is it priceless? What IS the price?*

His cell phone rings again.

"Hello. Yea. I hear ye," he shouts. "My partner told me you'd call. How's by you? How's the wife and kiddies?" (long pause)

"No way . . . No scratching the numbers. Hello . . . Hello . . . Arthur . . . Arthur . . . you there . . . you hear me? He hung up on me, the bastard!" he laments into thin air. The shoppers are not paying attention to him. The Woman is giving them a great show.

The spectators and sales employees continue their dance around The Woman. No one pays attention to The Man in the upholstered chair.

Suddenly the atmosphere changes. No longer does he sound pleasant, and in a gruff voice he bellows in our direction, "Wrap it up." The timing is right-on . . . ten minutes shy of the two allotted hours.

The Man slides off the chair, takes out his black American Express Card and hands it to the manager. The computer spits out the sales statement: $31,540.17. He looks at the bill and in his authoritative voice demands: "Gimme me a pen."

Joy . . . hugs . . . kisses all around.

Pen in hand, his phone rings again. He listens. His face turns red. His hands lose muscle control. The pen drops to the floor. The Man's face is puffing up . . . a balloon about to burst . . . his breath is labored.

"After . . . after all this, f*** time! Yeah, you gave your damn word . . . you're a liar . . . what do you mean you got involved in a Ponzi scheme? A Ponzi scheme? You . . .

no! Watch your knees . . . you slimy p***. We shook hands on the deal. Ninety-six mill! . . . Fork it over, . . . or I'll . . . I'll . . . sue you . . . I'll . . . Canceling a ninety-six million dollar order? What do you mean you haven't got it anymore? You . . . You . . . c***!" he screams. The Man slams the phone shut and shouts to the sales woman:

"CANCEL THE ORDER!" He faces his wife.

"Let's get the hell out of dis joint." He grabs The Woman's right hand and pushes her out the door. In his haste, he squeezes her hand hard. She loses her balance, trips and screams. Her "Knocker" is hurting her.

Some diamonds are painful.

CHUTZPA

"Hello." I spoke in a childish, sleepy voice into the phone. I'd been fast asleep . . . the ringing woke me.

"Hi, Helga. This is Ian. I'm at the Miami Airport. Please pick me up."

I squinted my eyes to get a better look at the clock on my nightstand. It was 1:19 a.m.!

"Ian? Ian? What are you doing calling me at this hour?"

"Oh . . . well . . . I entered a music competition in Miami. I need a place to stay and I thought of you. You're the only one I know who lives there."

<hr/>

That's *chutzpa*!

I had not seen or heard from Ian or his family in five years. His father was my former husband's first cousin. Ian wasn't even a blood relative! But I loved this unique family. Ian hoped that I, a fellow artist, would help him. He was right.

"Wait at the main entrance of the airport. It'll take me about a half an hour."

I have to get dressed and put some makeup on. I must be assertive, or he'll walk all over me.

"Don't move from the portico . . . I'm not parking my car . . . if you're not there when I arrive . . . I'll turn around . . . you'll be on your own."

Since Ian is such a nut, anything was possible. I didn't want to make the trip needlessly. Tomorrow was a workday. I needed my sleep. I'm a day person. Luckily at this ungodly hour there would be no traffic, except perhaps for a few lunatics on the road that Miami was so well-known for.

On the drive to the airport, I realized how upset I was. *The nerve of him! Waking me up the middle of the night . . . not calling in advance to ask IF he could stay with me. Did he think I was running a B&B? For goodness sakes . . . I, too, have a life!*

I'd moved to Miami in 1973, lived by myself and enjoyed it. During the past year I'd personally invited guests. But this situation was intrusive. I didn't like losing my power, but then . . . it's Ian . . . he's eccentric.

Ian was seven-years-old when I met him, his parents, and older brother. Al and I had become engaged. He wanted me to meet the other part of his family . . . the artsy ones. Of course Al knew I would love these cuckoo birds. The family members I had met previously were pleasant, but boring.

Ian's father, Aaron, was Al's first cousin. He was a well-known classical cellist who started his career at an early age playing with Arturo Toscanini's Symphony Orchestra for NBC radio in the 1940s. When I met him he was under contract with the impresario, Sol Hurok. His wife, a cellist, had dark, curly ringlets, an engaging smile and a well-rounded figure. I imagined her fitting into a cello case. Ian had an older brother, who played the French horn. However, he was determined not to be a musician like his zany family and became a mathematician.

What I'll remember forever of that first visit to Ian's home was hearing sophisticated scales being played before Al and I even got to the entrance of their house, where we were joyously greeted by the parents. Seven-year old Ian was at the grand piano. When he saw us, he immediately got off his stool, kicked the leg of the piano, and introduced himself. He bowed formally, and quickly returned to his playing. I was amazed, and thought . . . *He has good manners . . . that are incredibly mature for a seven-year old.* Ian continued to play, and each time he made an error he kicked the leg of the grand piano. When he played a Mozart piece, he became oblivious to his surroundings . . . that is until he heard kids outside shouting, "Ian, we need you!"

Instantly he scooted from the piano, ran to the front door, picked up his bat and glove from the floor, and ran out, slamming the door behind him. He was part of the baseball team! I was flabbergasted. What a dichotomy. This back and forth routine continued until the ninth inning. Ian, as if uninterrupted, continued practicing at the piano and kicking the leg whenever he hit a wrong key.

I was impressed with the dedication of such a young child. And as I looked around the living room I noticed besides the grand piano, five cellos, a couch, a bridge table and a few folding chairs. The décor was unexpected.

Seventeen years have passed since that performance. Ian graduated from the Julliard School of Music and also studied under the renowned teachers Madames Ania Dorfman, Rosina Lhevinne and Nadia Reisenberg. Competitions are important for aspiring solo artists and that is why Ian had come to the Miami Beach National Competition. He was twenty-four-years-old and this was his last chance to compete.

I picked up Ian at the airport and brought him to my one bedroom apartment, deciding that this was my opportunity to help a young ambitious artist. The next five days weren't easy. He was extremely demanding.

His first request, almost adamant, was, "Helga, I need a well-tuned piano immediately."

"Ian, I didn't expect you, and none of my friends have pianos. I'll make some phone calls in the morning, but don't count on it."

"Well, that doesn't sound promising." *That's not my fault.*

"And . . . oh . . . I'll also need your car." *He's insane! He's all about himself. Why hadn't he planned this in advance? Oh, I forgot . . . he's an artist!*

"Ian . . . I work . . . I need my car."

"Maybe you can get a ride from one of your friends."

"That's absolutely out of the question. You really have chutzpa! I have my work. There is no public transportation. You'll just have to rent a car. "

I can't believe his nerve. Ian has no concept of other people's needs . . . it's all about him. What did I let myself in for?

He was not happy; but he was lucky. One of my friends contacted someone who would be delighted to have a pianist in her apartment playing classical music for five days. And fortunately for Ian, she lived only four blocks away . . . he could walk there.

The next day I came home from work to my usually neat and well-kept apartment. I had been away for only a few hours, and in that time, the place was in shambles. Ian slept on the couch in the living room, which became a disaster area. His clothes and toilet articles were everywhere. He had allergies and the waste paper basket was overflowing with used tissues. It never occurred to him to empty the trash. I became his maid. I had to . . . I couldn't stand what I saw. On top of all the inconveniences, we shared the bathroom. I kept my cool thinking: *it will all be over in five days.*

There were two items of good news. He found the piano in "reasonably" good shape, and he was a good conversationalist, bright, with a great sense of humor. That made him an interesting dinner companion.

By coincidence my best friend Ruth, from Chile, whom I've known since we were five years old, was visiting me in Miami with her husband, a psychiatrist. It turned out that Ian was a "case" her husband would never forget.

I invited them to join Ian and me at dinner the first evening. I chose a restaurant that had good food, but more importantly . . . a piano bar. As we were escorted to our table and passed the piano, Ian couldn't resist walking over and lovingly stroke the instrument. When we were seated he appeared agitated. He kept looking at the piano, yearning to play, like a drug addict who needs his fix. The three-piece combo started to play. Ian was noticeably fidgeting in his seat. Finally he faced me and whispered, "Helga, could you talk to the manager and ask if I could play during the break?"

Did Ian think of me as his agent? I nodded in agreement, and did so. The combo leader looked at me doubtfully, but I assured him: "He's a professional . . . you'll be pleased." He allotted ten minutes.

When Ian got the sign to go on, he leaped from the chair and hurried to the piano stool, not wanting to waste any of his granted time. As soon as he started to play the diners stopped talking. I sensed anticipation, and then disbelief by the customers. This caliber of music was not expected at a piano bar. Ian was in his own world . . . eyes closed . . . in heaven. He surprised me by asking if I had a request. I took a chance, not knowing how he would react to my choice: Gershwin's *Rhapsody in Blue*. His rendition was outstanding. I thought about how lucky I was to be able to experience this performance. All the discomfort at home seemed worthwhile.

―――――

As the time came closer to the competition, Ian became increasingly nervous. For the night of the contest I planned an early home-cooked meal and invited Ruth and her husband to join us. We would all go to the concert together and drop Ian off early, at the stage entrance. The table was set. My friends were present. The food was ready. Ian wasn't. He told me he was too nervous to eat . . . he needed to meditate. We waited. There was plenty of time.

"Would you draw a hot bath for me . . . it would be relaxing?" I hadn't done that since my children were little . . . and they never asked me. Life is interesting. *Someday I'll write about these five days.*

While the water was running, Ian took out a crumbled navy blue suit from his duffel bag. It looked like it might have been from his Bar Mitzvah. What to do? It was Sunday . . . the cleaners were closed. I was nervous. The suit was in awful condition. My maternal instinct told me, *he couldn't go on stage looking like a Bowery Bum!*

Ian saw my distress and assured me, "Don't worry, Helga. Give me a hanger . . . I'll hang the suit above the bathtub. The steam will get the wrinkles out. I do it all the time."

Ruth, her husband, and I started to eat. Ian didn't want food. At that point, I didn't either. I had lost my appetite. *What if the suit falls into the bathtub?* After some time Ian appeared in the living room, dripping wet, with just a towel around his middle. He was in a panic . . . he couldn't find his razor. We all left the table to help in the search, which ended happily when the shaver was discovered under the couch.

A moment later another crisis arose . . . he couldn't find his bow tie. That was solved when he called his music director who luckily had an extra one. Still, the problems weren't over. Ian pulled his rumpled white shirt out of his duffel bag. I was willing to iron it, but I couldn't repair the frayed collar. Finally, when he was almost dressed . . . another problem . . . he had left his cuff links in New York! Ruth's husband came to the rescue . . . he had a pair at the hotel. *What's next?*

At Gusman Hall we left Ian at the stage door and wished him the usual "Break a leg." I felt as though I had dropped off my youngest child at daycare. Then after all the sartorial interruptions, we three breathed a simultaneous sigh of relief. I became nervous. There were ten participants, all wanting to be Number One. The quality of the talent was high. Sitting in the auditorium I had the feeling that

I was waiting for my offspring to perform. I was thrilled and proud when his name was called. Tears welled in my eyes.

Ian came out of the wing with downcast eyes . . . made no contact with the audience . . . he looked awkward. Like an old man he slowly shuffled onto the stage. I held my breath . . . he almost tripped over his shoes as he walked toward the piano. *Had he tied his laces?* When he got to the stool, he made adjustments, up and down, again and again. I was fidgeting in my seat watching him. It was ridiculous how long it took until he was satisfied, and finally sat down.

He raised his arms, and almost touched the keyboard. I assumed the performance was about to start. But no! His right hand went to his jacket left breast pocket. He took out a handkerchief and commenced to wipe all the piano keys! *This was not Victor Borge doing a comedy act.* When his "housekeeping" was done, he used the handkerchief to wipe his brow and with an unexpected dramatic flourish, swooped it back into in his pocket! He closed his eyes . . . waited . . . then . . . finally . . . commenced to play.

There was a hush in the audience. I sensed them wondering: *Does this clown know how to play?* And play he did: Mozart's *Rondo in A minor.* Tears rolled down my cheeks. Ian was in his own world, and it was glorious. There was tremendous applause. Ian bowed to the audience with his head down, like a fearful three-year-old, who doesn't want to look at you. I found it embarrassing to watch.

When the program came to a close, the conversation among the audience seemed to favor Ian as the outstanding performer. However, when the awards were announced,

Ian came in second. I heard rumors that he didn't get the First Prize because he lived in New York, not Florida.

———

Ian was devastated when he learned the result, and he asked me to accompany him to find a pay phone in the lobby. He called his mother. Her reaction to the news was: "No wonder you lost. I told you to play the Rachmaninoff." With tears in his eyes, he hung up. I put my arms around him. He cried like a baby.

———

For a number of years, following this episode, Ian and his father traveled in Europe where they concertized for several seasons, as well as one date in Carnegie Hall. The father-and-son duo never made it big-time, as hoped. Ian returned to New York where he gave private lessons.

In 1997, at the age of forty-eight, he took his Steinway and moved to Kansas City, where he became a stockbroker.

He's still there . . . with his Steinway.

Born to be Wild

I am a semi-retired New York fashion designer with forty years of experience. Some years ago, I worked part-time teaching clothing design at University of Miami and the International Fashion Institute. One of the courses I enjoyed most was teaching young, naïve students how to dress and comport themselves at job interviews.

Now, twenty years later, I'm sitting in the dentist's chair waiting for news about my x-rays. The good doctor comes in, but has a bad report. The price to repair my teeth is way beyond what I anticipated. I don't want to touch my savings. What to do? Get a job? I've enjoyed being self-employed for two decades; this will certainly be a major change for me.

My dentist's office at St. Armand's Circle, in Sarasota, is near a women's boutique shop I admire. I am practically there . . . I meander to the store. There is no HELP WANTED sign in the window. That's good. I'm certainly not dressed for an interview. Of all things, today I am wearing my favorite white tee shirt that I bought outside the Guggenheim Museum in Manhattan. In bold black letters it reads "Born to be Wild, New York," with a child-like cartoon-happy face wearing a red calico headband.

How can I go for an interview dressed like that? I can't. No way. At the same time I am thinking: *If I don't take the leap, I know I will not return at another time.* The pro and con conversations in my head are annoying.

Finally I decide to do it.

I will sell myself.

I take a deep breath and enter the shop. A smiling face greets me. I ask to see the manager.

The smiling face says, "That's me."

After a moment's conversation the manager asks me into her office. I apologize for the way I am dressed, and tell her that I love the merchandise in her store. She is impressed with me, and my experience. I'm hired on the spot.

So much for teaching proper interview attire.

Nothing Is Forever

He's dead. Sid is no more.

Nothing is forever.

I'd been thinking about him, and called the son of his oldest friend. I was informed that Sid died nine months ago, several days after his 94th birthday. Had I known, I would have gone to his memorial service. No one contacted me.

I knew it would end this way.

He was an unforgettable character.

It was 1980. I was taking a psychology course at the University of Miami. A woman whom I had met at a Gestalt seminar came to one session and by coincidence she was my teacher's companion. The following week my instructor asked me to stay after class. I wasn't a school child who had done something wrong, but rather a fifty-two year old woman taking a college course. From interaction in the class, the instructor knew that I was divorced but wanted to know if I was currently in a relationship. No. The request piqued my curiosity. The facilitator's girlfriend was a close friend of Sid's daughter, who had an "eligible" father. They decided that the two of us would be a good match. Would I permit Sid to call? Sure. But I wanted information about the man. The facts were immediately forthcoming: divorced, intelligent, amusing, good-looking, retired, and well-to-do. As they say in the Big Apple, "Not bad." And so it was . . . for many years.

The "bachelor" father was seventy-two, and I, twenty years his junior. However, I had no knowledge of his age until months later. My first impression of Sid as he stepped out of the elevator of my apartment building with his flashing smile, was positive. As he approached me, he waved both arms enthusiastically, like a sports enthusiast watching a touchdown. I thought, *now, here's a senior citizen with energy!* I returned the smile, and watched in amazement as he sprinted like a young kid to my front door. It was quite a performance. I was amused. He was short but made up for his stature, (5"5') by his good looks . . . full head of wavy silver hair, trimmed dark mustache, twinkling brown eyes, and a deep dimple in the middle of his chin . . . a George Clooney look-alike. (Years before GC became a movie idol.)

Sid looked like a dapper sixty-something, debonair, actor of the 1940s, and completing the image, he wore an ascot. Was he trying to impress me, the fashion designer, or did he dress in that manner as a general rule? As time passed, I became aware that he perceived himself to be four inches taller than he was. I thought of the diminutive, impulsive, bright Sid, as . . . *The Napoleon of Brooklyn.*

⸻

When his mother was pregnant with him in 1907, the family was poor. She had three teenage children to feed and clothe, and wanted an abortion. The lack of birth control at that time made the procedure commonplace, but also dangerous. Life can be unpredictable. Her contact was not available . . . she had used this person three times previously . . . and didn't trust anyone else. Six months later a robust healthy baby was born. His parents, brother, and two much older sisters, adored the baby. Sid was loved, cared for, and spoiled by women his entire life. No one was able to resist his charismatic street-wise brightness. His charm never wavered . . . even into his nineties. He was unique, and so was his life.

⸻

Sid adored his father . . . unconditionally. The family of six was either poor or flush, depending on what his father did to earn a living at the moment. When money ran out, he would suddenly leave for long extended periods of time. No one ever questioned his whereabouts, or where his money came from. At the beginning of every departure there were enough resources to feed the family, but after several weeks, (he always seemed to stay away longer than anticipated) things got precarious. His mother became inventive . . . a whiz at preparing potatoes in interesting ways to avoid hearing, "Is That All There Is?"

Everyone was always fascinated by Sid's stories of his early life. When he was a little boy and there was nothing to eat . . . the family was starving . . . suddenly the door would burst open in their fourth-floor walk-up apartment, and there, in all his glory, the exalted father had returned . . . laden with four large gift-wrapped boxes . . . one for each of his children. When he came home, there was always a grand entrance. He dug deep into his jacket and pants pockets and dramatically threw wads and wads of paper money on the kitchen table . . . toward his wife . . . for all to see. Father was a showman and played the role well.

Little Sid adored him. Here was his Messiah. It was not the money that interested Sid; he wanted to see what was in the boxes. This time, before Easter, coinciding with the Passover Seder when the Messiah is invited, was the returning father with four gigantic, larger than life size, chocolate Easter Bunnies! The family hadn't eaten properly for days. Sid bit into the chocolate with a vengeance . . . couldn't stop and devoured the whole thing within the hour. Of course he became ill . . . but who cared? . . . his father was home!

The young boy trailed him whenever possible . . . he couldn't get enough of him. Even at a young age, the little tyke always surmised that in a short time, his adoring father would be gone again. Whenever Sid so eloquently told and retold that story, I looked at his face and saw the love for his hero . . . his father. I visualized these characters in silent films and, of course, thought of Charlie Chaplin.

On another occasion, the Messiah came home from one of his "trips." It was an unbearable hot July day in

Brooklyn. He told his wife that a great surprise was in store for the entire family. She was ordered to pack the family's clothes for an extended time, and to be ready to leave the apartment in an hour.

The children hastily gathered some of their things, dumped them into the well-used cardboard suitcases, and tied them with re-used cord. From the top of the stairs they shoved the valises down the four flights, and finally, out of the building to the sidewalk. What was the surprise? Papa had rented a huge Bentley convertible complete with a chauffeur! It was parked at the sidewalk. Papa was rich again. The family was going to a hotel in the Catskill Mountains, in grand style. They stayed there much of that glorious, hot, summer until the money ran out. And on the return trip to Brooklyn, there was no Bentley . . . just a broken-down hack that took them back to reality . . . and Brooklyn. (A hack was an unlicensed large car, used as a taxi for long excursions.) The interior had ample room for three, plus two fold-up leather-upholstered seats, and accommodations for two passengers next to the driver . . . that made it seven. Usually there were kids on the adult's laps as well. Of course, no seatbelts.

Sid was intelligent and street smart. At sixteen, he graduated from high school with honors. For years during the Great Depression he took any job available. At night he went to CCNY, studying accounting. It was the right profession for a young man who loved to make and spend money. He had inherited his father's passion for high living.

During the day he worked as a delivery boy for Milgrim's, one of the first exclusive woman's boutique shops on West 57th Street. The good-looking young man was well liked. He quickly learned that Uptown Manhattan was very different from Brooklyn. Sid appreciated the difference. With his eyes wide open, his tastes changed.

He married a young schoolteacher. Financially, times were tough, and the young newly-weds shared a tiny apartment with another married couple. When his son David, a beautiful baby, was born, a way had to be found to provide for his growing family. Sid's brother, ten years his senior, was working as a "bookie." The money was good, but illegal. During the Depression, desperate people gambled their last nickel. It gave them some hope . . . someone had to win . . . why not them? His brother enticed Sid to join him. It sounded exciting. Within a short time, with money in his pocket, Sid inveigled his brother to let him become a partner . . . suggesting that the brothers open their own bookmaking business.

An entrepreneur was in the making. Young Sid had great ideas. They specialized in sporting events, primarily horseracing. He respected his brother and insisted theirs would be a 50/50 partnership. A suitable location in New Jersey was found, and a dozen people manned the phones. The site constantly changed in order not to be caught by the police. People had to be bribed . . . the business thrived . . . money poured in. He loved the excitement of the mayhem. Years later, when I got to know Sid well; I realized he would have loved to be have been born into a Mafia family. Sid had friends who were part of that establishment and found them loyal to each other.

The young entrepreneur became rich. When his wife gave birth to a girl, Miriam, he bought a large house in Sea Gate, an upper middle class community, facing the Atlantic Ocean. Sid loved the excitement, the money, and the wonderful location for his family home. No more four-flight walk-ups. Now he could rub elbows with the other nouveau riche. In his largesse, he was generous to all his family. They came to him when they needed money. Their requests were always granted. The family man was in charge . . . he had power . . . he felt good.

———

Suddenly it all stopped.

They got caught. The devoted brothers were arrested and sent to jail. Gregarious Sid, who loved to tell stories and told them well, never spoke about this chapter in his life. The smart Brooklyn kid got caught . . . was embarrassed . . . changed his name . . . sold his lovely house . . . and sent his family to Miami Beach where no one knew their background. The brothers were incarcerated. A new beginning was on the horizon.

———

In time he was freed, and his family moved back to New York, with the children grown by now. His son David was extremely handsome and had his father's charisma. He adored Sid, but aside from his physical attributes and his father's charm, he had no focus, no direction. Quite by chance, at a party, David met some Hollywood moguls.

They were smitten by his good looks, and he was invited to Tinseltown where they gave him a small part in the movie, "High Wind in Jamaica," starring Anthony Quinn and Sterling Hayden.

His charm and natural acting ability led to another movie offer. However, he declined. A drifter was born. David became deeply involved in drugs and moved to Mexico. Sid was adamant about persuading his son to give up the habit. He was so concerned that he followed him to Mexico. After living with David for six months, Sid reluctantly gave up his effort to help him. It was futile. At twenty-nine, David died of an overdose. Sid was devastated; so much so, that he didn't attend his beloved son's funeral.

Sid was informed that there was a woman and a child in his son's life. In his grief he didn't follow through . . . wanted no connection. Sid was guilt-ridden, and blamed himself for David's death. He never got over it.

He divorced his first wife.

A few years later, luck caught up with Sid again. An internationally known gambling casino hired him for their finance department in Paradise Island, the Bahamas. He bought a sailboat, docked it five hundred feet from the casino entrance, and walked to work.

Paradise returned.

When Sid was a young man, he fell in love with sailboats. One glorious summer day when he was driving on Long Island, the bridge went up to let a sailboat through. Dozens of vehicles had to stop. At first Sid, who was short on patience, was annoyed, but as he waited, he became amused. He liked the idea that a little sailboat can stop progress. Power . . . even when small. A short time after that revelation, he bought his first boat from a newspaper advertisement. Sid and a friend traveled all the way to Lake George to see the gem. On sight, he bought the boat. Without any sailing experience, but lots of chutzpa, the two men sailed home to Brooklyn.

By sheer luck, they returned to New York without incident. Realizing how fortunate they were, Sid took sailing lessons and became excellent at the craft. His first boat turned out to be a lemon, but the experience taught him to be more selective. However, being an impulsive person, he wasn't always successful. In his lifetime Sid owned sixteen boats in varying sizes, from fourteen to eighty-six feet, and remembered the name of each one. That was not the case when trying to remember the names of his many girlfriends. When that subject came up, he laughed, but his daughter didn't.

Sid never gambled, except with his life. Working in the casino and with his experience as a bookie, he knew that "the house" eventually wins. Even though gamblers and the Mafia surrounded him, he didn't drink or smoke. However, he was a womanizer. He was particularly attracted to beautiful married women. Did he want to get caught, or did he just love the excitement? His desire to tell me about his past lovers was not of interest to me. As a matter of fact, I found the boasting totally immature. I especially abhorred how he tricked his wife into believing that he was a caring father by taking his little five-year old daughter to the circus. The child was with him not to show the public that he was a good daddy, but to meet one of his paramours, who came with her child and a baby sitter, who acted as the "beard." I wasn't curious about stories of his love life, but by then, he was in his eighties, and I, he said, was his "Last Hurrah." That statement hooked me. Sometimes I listened.

In a short time Sid was promoted to credit manager at the casino. That position gave him the authority to give or deny credit to the international customers . . . the "hooked" gamblers. There were incredible stories he related about well-known, influential people, lawyers, doctors, politicians, CEOs, and of course show business personalities, who degraded themselves by begging him for more credit . . . after losing fortunes. Little Sid loved the power of being The Big Chief.

Another turning point in his life occurred when he met a woman dining alone in a restaurant. The bon vivant introduced himself, and within two days she was living with Sid on his boat. A week later they married. His womanizing stopped.

After a few years he decided that he had accumulated enough money for the rest of his life and retired. He was generous with his fortune . . . giving freely to the people he loved. Sid decided to continue to live on his boat. His religion, he said, was being a Jewish sailor from Brooklyn. Living in the Bahamas was the perfect opportunity to buy another sailboat.

Heaven was close by.

———

Virgin Gorda was his favorite port of call. He lived there with his new wife for three years. It is a tiny, beautiful, mountainous island with one little charming hotel, an amazingly fine restaurant, and a handful of houses. The highlight of the week was Wednesday when fresh baked goods were delivered by boat. That was a far cry from his background, living in New York City, where everything is available day and night.

———

On one of our many sailing trips, he took me to Virgin Gorda. As we approached the harbor, with Sid at the helm, I heard joyous shouts of, "Little Sid is back!" He hadn't been there in years, but once you met Sid, you didn't forget him. The dock master was thrilled to see him again. I was impressed with the island's beauty . . . but to live there? Sid's explanation when I asked how he occupied his time living in such tight quarters on a picture perfect beautiful island, where there was nothing much to do . . . no movies or theaters . . . just a few new people who docked near him from time to time, was simple, "Every three months I flew into Manhattan with my wife to get my 'fix,' . . . staying at the Gotham Hotel for ten days, seeing all the Broadway shows, art exhibits, visiting friends and family."

Shopping was not his thing, but stocking up on good books to bring back to the boat was. He mentioned that if he didn't have money to take a break four times a year to New York, he would not have survived the life on the boat. When I asked him how his wife occupied her daily routine, he had a peculiar look on his face and said, "I haven't a clue." I was shocked.

After several years, he divorced his second wife. (Don't know why.)

He never saw her again.

The sailor moved back to Miami Beach after living on his various sailboats for sixteen years. He bought an old, architecturally interesting house facing Biscayne Bay where he had space to dock two sailboats, a fifty-six, and a lovely sixteen foot catboat, named *Spirit*. His daughter, Miriam, and her companion lived with him. He loved the house on the bay and having the luxury of his two sailboats docked outside his back yard. The larger boat was for serious sailing, and the small one was his toy. Sid was able to take the catboat for a spin by himself whenever he was in the mood, which was almost daily.

Life was great.

But nothing is forever.

New excitement found him. A real estate agent knocked on his door and informed Sid that she had a buyer for his house at triple the price he had just recently paid. The announcement was a total surprise. In his life, Sid had often been at the right place at the right time, and this was a perfect example.

As much as he loved his house, Sid could not resist the enormous windfall. Everything had its price. Within two weeks he rented a two-bedroom apartment, and a houseful of furniture was piled on top of each other, until he bought his next house.

Shades of his father?

The impulsive Sid immediately bought a lovely villa on the opposite side of town but not near enough to the Miami waterways for his two sailboats. He sold the large boat, kept *Spirit,* and rented a private dock for her. It was an inconvenient arrangement, but he had the money. Impulsive Sid didn't do his research. His daughter and her companion weren't concerned . . . they were living rent-free in Sid's new house. Everyone was happy.

Serendipity was often on Sid's side. Sometime previous to the unexpected house profit, he had contacted his stockbroker on the advice of a friend who had given him a hot tip. Sid decided to invest a large percentage of his money in the market. The broker did as he was told, and in a short time the stock took off. That was no surprise to Sid, except . . . he had given the broker the wrong company name, which sounded similar. The incorrect transaction turned into another bonanza!

At the beginning of our relationship, Sid was fun to be with. I had never known anyone with his personality. His enthusiasm and energy were boundless and exciting. Although retired, he was never bored. We both enjoyed reading and the arts. I loved cooking and entertaining our many friends. Of course Sid had his sailboat. I thought of *Spirit* as his pet . . . a dog substitute. The similarity was the same; his catboat was always there for him just as the women in his life had been. However, the ladies never gave him chores . . . they pampered him. He literally didn't know what went on in a kitchen. *Spirit* was different. Sid lovingly tended to her needs no matter how difficult or time consuming. Sailing brought out the free spirit in him. He had an enthusiastic audience for his many astonishingly true scenarios.

Now that we were together, he had a new audience. Sid was a true storyteller, which made each repeated account fresh (for me). He also loved to dance and play the piano . . . loud, and badly. Always the center of attraction, he was a true Leo the Lion.

Sid brought out the child in me, which was a good thing since I, the Virgo, was too serious. He claimed I gave him the grounding that he needed. In spite of our personality differences, we were compatible . . . most of the time. Some of his values shocked me. I reasoned: *no one's perfect.* After seeing each other for six months, Sid suggested that we live together.

I knew my parents would never have approved. He would have been an embarrassment to them. How could they explain to their friends that their properly brought up Jewish daughter was living with a former bookie and . . . out of wedlock? However, that was not a concern to me at this time since they were no longer alive. Truthfully, twenty years earlier I would not have been attracted to Sid . . . he was not my type! But, now at fifty-two, it was time for me to have fun . . . to be entertained.

I was free.

My new companion wanted to buy a large sailboat for us to live on. Immediately I put my foot down. No way! I'm a land person, and need my beautiful surroundings, especially walls for artwork. Also, I had my own fashion-design business and worked six days a week. Weekend sailing suited me just fine. Truthfully I loved when it rained, since then we went out to dinner and a movie, which I preferred to sailing. But I kept quiet. As much as Sid loved his sailboat, I loved my sophisticated apartment . . . swimming pool facing Biscayne Bay . . . full view of Miami Beach . . . the twinkling lights at night . . . and the most glorious sunrises.

We solved our problem. Sid moved into my apartment but not until I made my requirements very clear. I agreed to live with him but only if all our expenses; rent, food and entertainment were to be shared 50/50. I had no intention of being *a kept woman*. My business was growing and I was independent. *Spirit* had a free dock slip where we lived, and Sid was able to see his boat from our terrace.

Neither of us was interested in marriage. I wanted no legal entanglement. That knowledge felt good. We were on my turf. The arrangement was as perfect as it could be. All the furnishings and artwork were mine . . . nothing changed, except I gave up a closet, and a man was living with me in my apartment.

Paradise.

My children liked Sid, and Sid's daughter, Miriam, heartily approved of me. No wonder. Sid had dated women younger than she, and now, here was I, a mature, self-confident, independent feminist. It was the first time in her father's life that he did chores in the house. (Why is it so difficult to teach men to throw out the garbage? I never totally succeeded.)

Miriam was very close to her father, but that had not been the case when she was younger. Her brother was the handsome one whom her father loved. David looked like a taller version of his dad . . . but she? She was homely as a young child . . . unattractive as an adult. It was impossible for Sid to comprehend that his child wasn't beautiful. Good looks were exceedingly important to him. I didn't like those values and called him on it. "Sid, not everyone is lucky enough to be born beautiful." Besides, he couldn't believe that Miriam wasn't smart. It was difficult for him to realize that his wife, a schoolteacher, and he, an accountant, had produced such a being.

The child had been frustrated, unhappy, struggled in school and almost didn't graduate from high school. But she WAS smart and took it upon herself when she became a teenager to go into therapy, although her father didn't believe in it. Her problem was diagnosed; dyslexia. With that knowledge, she bloomed in school, and graduated from college with honors. It was after her brother died, that Sid re-discovered his long, lost daughter.

Early in our relationship Sid and I got into an argument that changed the way we traveled by car. He was a "cowboy driver." Behind the wheel, this man was a demon and berated everyone on the road, especially seniors. Ridiculous. I vividly remember the incident that precipitated who drove who, what, and where. We were going to the theater, Sid was driving and had his eye on a spot in the parking lot; another person had the same idea. He revved up the engine and almost collided with the other car. Both drivers luckily stopped in time but neither was polite enough to move. They just sat, glaring at each other through their windshields and didn't give an inch. I became upset because there were other spots available but headstrong Sid, and his antagonist were too stubborn to give in. I voiced my opinion. It was ignored. Sid was steaming and breathing heavily. After what seemed like forever, I opened the car door and proceeded to get out.

"Where are you going?" Sid wanted to know.

"You can continue to be stubborn and sit in the parking lot, but I'm going to the theater, with or without you!" I opened my purse, and threw his theater ticket in his lap. He got the point and immediately found another parking spot.

"In the future, we either go in two cars, or I drive," I told him.

"Great! Now I have a chauffeur." (He was so clever.)

Sid used to laugh at himself about his bad sense of direction. He literally got lost going to the airport where he had been dozens of times. But at sea, the man never made an error. When we traveled in the Caribbean, I was impressed; he recognized every landmark and every little island that he had ever been to. He would look through the binoculars and get excited, like a child, when he saw a familiar guidepost 'way in the distance. At sea he never got lost.

One perfectly glorious summer afternoon we were sailing in the Caribbean on his nephew Ken's fifty-eight foot *Dove*. The boat was custom built in Norway, and Sid and his nephew flew to Europe to sail the boat on its maiden voyage to Long Island. At age ten Ken had been taught to sail by his Uncle Sid. Years later he won the prestigious Bermuda Race with his *Dove,* and gave the credit to Sid.

One sea journey is unforgettable. We were five congenial people on board Ken's fifty-eight-foot sailboat. Everyone was on deck except Carol, the nephew's wife. She was below, reading. I was daydreaming. The mild winds suddenly picked up . . . the boat was heeling. The roar was frightening to me. (I can still hear it thirty years later.) I imagined suddenly falling into the sea. Everyone except me knew that was a common summer weather pattern in the Caribbean.

The three men got into action immediately. They scurried around like mice out of a hole . . . pushing . . . flinging anything that was in their way . . . shouting commands over the roar of the astonishing noise . . . running around to get to one of the sails that had ripped. I had heard it, but didn't know what it was and just imagined a catastrophe. It was torturous. Adjustments had to be made quickly. The boat rocked from side to side, the wind continued to howl.

I was cursing . . . unusual for me . . . although no one could hear me. I realize now, that I enjoyed "spitting" out those four letter words . . . it loosened my frustration. Isolated in my little space . . . clutching my hands on the railing . . . holding on for dear life . . . I was shouting to the sky, "Who the * . . . needs this . . . why does anyone want to sail . . . why be so uncomfortable . . . can't even go to the toilet comfortably . . . or take a long shower . . . they are all nuts . . . a wasted vacation . . . give me a hotel and land . . . I will never do this again!" I could hardly breathe. I was frightened and exhausted.

Carol came from below and saw my anguish. I was nauseated. She immediately brought me a bucket and chunks of dry bread. Her advice: "Force yourself to eat the bread . . . take deep breaths . . . remove your white knuckled fingers from the railing . . . keep breathing." She assured me that the men knew what they were doing. "I give you my word . . . you will not fall into the sea."

The men seemed to enjoy the excitement and thrived at the decisions they had to make. The volume of the shouted commands above the noise of the howling wind unnerved me.

As suddenly as the storm came upon us . . . it subsided. Everything was beautiful again . . . like natural childbirth. (There is pain, but after the baby miraculously appears, the agony is forgotten.) This was a horrific experience. Sid and I came to a simple agreement; we would alternate our many vacations between land and sea.

Sid was proud of my talents. A year before we met, I had gone into my own business, designing and manufacturing women's clothing under my own label. Through sales representatives, my line of clothing was sold throughout the United States and in some Caribbean islands. I was extremely flattered and touched when he offered to invest in my enterprise and happily agreed to a working partnership.

I was adamant that I would be the boss of my firm. He wanted a 50/50 partnership. But since I knew the business and worked six days a week, and Sid only came to check the books on Fridays, I demanded 60/40. (I should have suggested 70/30, but I was too timid.) I looked to the future . . . if Sid died before me . . . he was two decades my senior . . . his share would go to his daughter. Miriam was a teacher who liked clothes but knew nothing about the garment business. I liked her, but I had to make sure I had voting power. Sid graciously agreed to my terms.

He willingly was the *schlepper* for my company. He took boxes to UPS, delivered special orders to local customers, and drove with me to many parts of Florida where I showed my line. We made mini-vacations out of some of the trips to Georgia and Las Vegas. I disliked that artificial city, but I was successful in selling my designs. He was a happy go-fer. One day after making a local delivery to a client, he returned with that irresistible devilish look in his eyes . . . like a little boy anxious to blurt out his story. The boutique owner couldn't resist the short, elderly deliveryman, dressed in his tightly well-tailored jeans, the black muscle shirt and the sexy dimple in his chin. She tipped him! He graciously accepted. Sid beamed when he related the story, and said, "Wait until the 'boys hear this one!"

As the business grew, I hired help. Sid, with his expertise in high finance, came once a week to check on mine. It worked well . . . until one day when I walked into the office. My partner was on the phone with a customer whose payment was in arrears. He was shouting into the phone, in a throaty voice, to my client, threatening her, "If you don't pay up within forty-eight hours, you'll have two broken knees!"

It was like a scene out of "The Godfather!" I was furious. I instantly wanted to throw him out . . . but he was my partner. "How dare you speak to my customers this way? You are not the Mafia!"

He glared at me.

"You are never to call my customers again."

Sid argued, "You'll be sweet . . . you'll lose your shirt . . . you'll never get paid."

"Sid, I'll get honey with honey. If I lose . . . I lose . . . but I'll be able to sleep at night. I will not permit intimidation." He backed off.

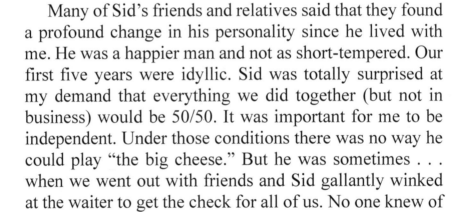

Many of Sid's friends and relatives said that they found a profound change in his personality since he lived with me. He was a happier man and not as short-tempered. Our first five years were idyllic. Sid was totally surprised at my demand that everything we did together (but not in business) would be 50/50. It was important for me to be independent. Under those conditions there was no way he could play "the big cheese." But he was sometimes . . . when we went out with friends and Sid gallantly winked at the waiter to get the check for all of us. No one knew of our financial arrangement and under the circumstances I paid half of the bill. If my friends had known they would not have permitted Sid's "generosity."

I loved my business and Sid had his sailboat and male friends. We both loved the arts, our friends, relatives, and the physical beauty of Miami. I loved making dinner parties, and Sid was in his milieu as the gracious host telling his amusing and fascinating stories. My enterprise was doing well. Sid suggested that we move into a large, two bedroom penthouse apartment, in the same building. It had a breathtaking view of Biscayne Bay, and the night-lights of Miami were magical. We would be able to accommodate over-night guests. I agreed.

It was perfect.

———

Five years into our relationship, I saw a change in Sid that made me unhappy. I needed to talk to someone. The perfect opportunity presented itself. We spent a long weekend in Philadelphia with Sid's nephew, Paul, a well-known, highly respected psychologist. I had been to one of his workshops. His style impressed me. I knew him as a good friend, and as Sid's surrogate son. There was a close bond between them. When we arrived, I approached Paul, asking him to set some time aside for me . . . I had to speak to him about his uncle. Shortly, he escorted me into his study, a comfortable den with cozy couches, chairs and interesting art. I started to relate my grievances, when Paul stopped me. He suggested inviting his uncle into the room in order for Sid to hear my problems . . . first hand. I agreed.

It was the most productive therapy session I'd ever experienced. Sid was upset about my unhappiness. He had no inkling about the numerous problems I had concerning him. To my surprise he was absolutely willing to rectify them. I learned an important lesson from Paul: Don't assume that people are mind readers.

We shouldn't presume that even the people closest to us know what we want. Sid had many talents, but being a mind reader was not one of them. At the end of the session we cried and hugged. He promised to be more aware of my needs, and I promised not to hide my complaints from him.

I felt guilty. Here was a man, in his late seventies, apologizing and promising to "be good." I reasoned to Paul . . . "I'm twenty years his junior . . . I don't want to admonish him."

"He's strong. Don't be afraid to tell him what is bothering you. Sid won't have a heart attack and die because you reprimand him."

Our solution didn't last long. Sid was good for a while, and then the "little boy" forgot again. I felt like his mommy with a naughty child. My mother's voice crept into my head telling me to respect my elders.

But she didn't live with Sid!

One day Sid spoke about his parents and realized that they had lived into their nineties. That disturbed him. He talked about . . . what if he lived another decade or two, and the money he had accumulated wasn't sufficient to support him in the life style he wanted? The thought depressed him. Sid found a solution.

He would go to work!

What type of employment would be suitable for a man of his age? With that in mind, Sid lost no time and went to the most prestigious marine yard in Miami. At the interview he related his sailboat experiences and was hired on the spot. He was given a lovely office overlooking Biscayne Bay. It was a joy to see him so ecstatic. The fact that he was on straight commission didn't concern him. Who knew more about sailboats than he . . . he's had sixteen?

His fantasy? He, the septuagenarian, would sell more sailboats than any of the other agents . . . half his age! His knowledge, experience and charisma worked to his advantage. It was refreshing to see him go to work with such enthusiasm. The company printed business cards . . . he was given an expense account and encouraged to take perspective buyers to lunch or dinner.

Lucky Sid . . . he'll have a new audience for his boating stories. The clients were so charmed by him . . . they invited him to their homes for dinner and at restaurants in many cases picked up the tab! He felt fulfilled.

Months passed. He always came home exhilarated with the knowledge of his impending sales. Sid had many "almost" . . . "for sure" deals. Unfortunately they never materialized. He was no salesman. When I saw what was happening I gave him a book, "Closing the Sale."

I should have guessed . . . he never looked at it . . . refused to discuss my suggestions. The potential clients lost interest in his never-ending stories. Needless to say, he never got to "closing the deal." Eventually, the clients bought elsewhere. Several wanted to remain friends, but Sid was embarrassed by his failure.

Finally he made a sale . . . to friends of my children who had fallen in love with an old wooden fifty-eight foot clunker of a sailboat. Sid warned them of the pitfalls and tried to persuade them not to buy it. They were young and stubborn. He was upset knowing the boat was not seaworthy. The couple persisted and bought the vessel from him. Sid refused to take a commission. The sailboat was transported from Jacksonville. We boarded the boat in Miami and sailed it to Sarasota. The ship was like an old fat, loving grandmother . . . slow, friendly and cozy.

This was Sid's only sale in eighteen months. He was asked to vacate his office.

He was devastated.

Sid and I went to Asia on one of our many land vacations. We were invited to be houseguests by friends of his who lived in Hong Kong, and by another in Singapore. I had met them several times in Miami and in the Caribbean and liked them. For me this would be a trip of a lifetime. With much enthusiasm I suggested that we include one week in Japan. How could I not visit Tokyo and Kyoto when I'm "in the neighborhood?" That suggestion didn't thrill Sid. He stated that he had been there years ago and had seen it all. Seen it all? How? While in Tokyo for two days he had hired a car and chauffeur . . . and saw the highlights through the car window! Sid loved to sail, fly and ride, but hated to walk. I pointed out that with me he would see the REAL Tokyo and Kyoto . . . using subways . . . buses and stopping to investigate places of interest. He agreed. I recommended that he take books with him, in case of boredom. "No problem," he said.

On a beautiful, clear, sunny Sunday in May of 1985, we took the subway to Jedo Park in Tokyo, a large, magnificently designed park with a zoo, museum and fabulous gardens. It reminded me of the Golden Gate Park in San Francisco. Happily it was a pleasant walk from the subway, which in itself was an interesting experience. The park was well attended by prosperous looking adults with beautiful well-behaved children. Sid was rewarded. A large banner covered the upper part of the entrance to the museum advertising . . . FRENCH IMPRESSIONISM . . . Sid's favorite period. I was thrilled . . . these were paintings that had never been seen outside of the Louvre. He would be satisfied. We entered the building and found it packed with people . . . like rush hour in New York City. Sid galloped through the exhibit . . . pulling me by the hand.

"Let's get out of here."

"No way!" I exclaimed. I never saw him walk so quickly. In record time we were out of the building. He was ready to leave the park . . . he had seen it all!

"Sid, this is a one-time opportunity. I only saw a blur. Please . . . take a book . . . sit on a bench in the beautiful flower garden . . . I'm going back inside." I wasn't going to let him spoil this adventure.

We had another surprise. The world-renowned Tokyo Zoo had just received a panda; the first in Japan. I had never seen one, and was very excited. Sid couldn't have cared less but was willing to take a look. Little did we know that everyone in the park had the same idea. It was a long walk from the museum. When Sid saw the crowd, he wanted to leave, but it was too late. We were pushed into a throng of enthusiastic people, anxious to see this cuddly, wide-eyed, furry sweet animal. It was a one-way road with no turning back.

Sid felt himself caught in the middle and grumbled like a spoiled little child. It became a mob scene; the line moved very slowly. Everyone, except Sid, wanted to see the pandas. The shy animal was hidden by bamboo and hardly moved, and neither did the line. The throng pushed us ahead and out of the area, into the open space of the zoo. My companion was exhausted and unhappy. We found a place to relax and have ice cream. Sweets always made Sid feel better.

Finally, we were ready to leave the park and find our way to the subway and then the hotel. Life is not that simple. The park is enormous and although I had a map, we got lost. I was sick of Sid's complaints . . . and approached several Japanese people for directions. They were gracious, smiled politely, but weren't able to communicate and that led us around in circles. We continuously came back to square one. At this point Sid became the "Ugly American," complaining that the Japanese don't understand English.

"Really, Sid? You're unfair. How do you think Japanese tourists feel when they're in New York, not understanding English, asking for directions? You're impossible."

He kept quiet. it was getting late and I was getting concerned about his well-being. I approached a young adult who was delighted to practice his English, and gave us proper directions. All was well again. I had anticipated unpleasantries on this trip. My premonition was right; yet the irritants were worth the experience.

There is no free lunch.

As time passed, Sid became more impatient. He lost interest in world happenings, became extremely negative and short-tempered. Except for the people he cared about, he considered everyone else stupid and unworthy. This man, who I had met nine years ago, was not the same Sid. I didn't like him anymore, not even as a casual friend and yet didn't have it in my heart to call it quits. He had always been good to me. I heard my mother's voice again, "Respect your elders." However, I had lost my respect for him.

And then the bomb dropped.

"I should have taken more . . . I wouldn't be in the position I'm in now . . . if I had." What was Sid talking about?

"When I was working with my friend at the casino, we each skimmed $5,000 a day. It was so easy. When I thought I had enough money for the rest of my life, I stopped. I was so proud of myself . . . my friend continued to work for the casino another year. I should have listened to him. I didn't know I was going to live this long."

I was stunned. Sid was boasting . . . as if to say, *See, I was nice, I stopped . . . I didn't over-do-it . . . they were so stupid . . . they never missed the money . . . there was so much.* Sid kept talking . . . as if to finally get it out of his system. He trusted me and continued to explain that he and his friend each had a key to the secured room that contained the vault. The two were entrusted with the repository combination number.

It was hard for me to deal with that *truth*. The situation had occurred many years ago, but this was the person I was living with. I told him how I felt. In my eyes he was not clever. Although he didn't hurt people . . . he stole . . . big time.

I told him, "You were a crook . . . lucky you didn't get caught. They could have hung you!" Sid sulked.

―――

In the last six months of our life together, I admonished him two more times. He always gave me an apology. I did a lot of soul-searching and came to the conclusion that I didn't like him, even as a roommate. He boasted that he had shielded me from some illegal things he had been involved with. I was furious. Fortunately we had no legal ties. I also knew that if I told Sid to leave, he would go back to his house where his daughter and son-in-law still lived. He would not be alone.

―――

"Sid, I've torn my closet apart and can't find my camera case. It's always on the top shelf, on the right, but it's not there. Come and help me."

"Don't worry, I have it."

"Why do you have it? What for? You don't have a camera."

"I needed it for something," he said.

"I don't understand what you needed it for. And why didn't you put it back where it belonged?"

He tried to explain. "Last month when I went on the business trip to California, I needed it; I had to put something in it."

I couldn't believe what I figured out. How could he do that, and with my property?

"What if you had been caught . . . my camera case has my name in it . . . I could have been implicated. Didn't you think of that?"

"I'm sorry."

I was so, so, angry . . . I had had it and said, "OUT! . . . NO MORE!"

Sid was a proud man. I knew he wouldn't linger. The following day he packed his personal belongings. I said I hoped we would stay on speaking terms. He replied, "I will not be your friend, but I will never be your enemy."

He left the apartment and returned to his home. No woman had ever said good-bye to Sid before. I was the first, and the last, to reject him. Neither he nor his daughter wanted any communication with me. Miriam was furious . . . after ten worry free years, she now had to deal with her father directly, under his roof.

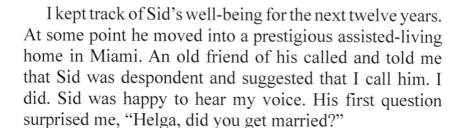

I kept track of Sid's well-being for the next twelve years. At some point he moved into a prestigious assisted-living home in Miami. An old friend of his called and told me that Sid was despondent and suggested that I call him. I did. Sid was happy to hear my voice. His first question surprised me, "Helga, did you get married?"

I laughed.

Sid had a motto: "Nothing Is Forever."

Memories are.

Biography

Helga Harris was born in Berlin, Germany, and moved with her family to New York City in 1938. As a young child she dreamed of being a fashion designer. She attended Brooklyn College and graduated from Pratt Institute. Helga achieved her goal and worked as designer in the fashion industry for forty years.

She moved to Miami in 1973, where she had her own fashion label. Helga taught fashion design at the University of Miami, and Bauder Fashion College. After moving to Sarasota in 1990, she was a design instructor at The Sarasota Vocational Technical School. Throughout her life Helga painted and has had numerous art exhibits in New York; especially at the Greenwich Village Outdoor Art Show where she exhibited for fifteen years. After moving to Sarasota she had many showings of her collages.

For the past fifteen years writing has become an important part of her creative life. Her memoir, *Dear Helga, Dear Ruth,* was published, as have several articles in *The Petersburg Times*, *The Sarasota Herald Tribune* and

The Tampa Tribune. Helga has contributed stories to anthologies, including *Dolls Remembered, Doorways*, and various magazines. The most recent collection, *We Were There,* was published by the St. Petersburg Holocaust Museum. She completed another memoir, *Susie . . . WAIT!*

Nothing Is Forever is Helga's first collection of nonfiction short stories.

Helga Harris is a Co-Leader in a writing program at The Lifelong Learning Academy. (USF)